Going to Live
in Italy

D0543560

Practical books that inspire

Going to Live in France
How to prepare for a successful visit, be it short, long-term, or forever

Living & Working in Paris
Your first-hand introduction to Paris and the Parisians

Teaching Abroad
How and where to find teaching and lecturing jobs worldwide

Retire Abroad
Your guide to a full and happy retirement in a foreign country

Send for a free copy of the latest catalogue to:

How To Books
3 Newtec Place, Magdalen Road,
Oxford OX4 1RE, United Kingdom
email: info@howtobooks.co.uk
http://www.howtobooks.co.uk

Going to Live in Italy

Your practical guide to life and work in Italy

AMANDA HINTON

3rd edition

howtobooks

Published by How To Books Ltd
3 Newtec Place, Magdalen Road
Oxford OX4 1RE, United Kingdom
Tel: (01865) 793806.   Fax: (01865) 248780.
email: info@howtobooks.co.uk
http://www.howtobooks.co.uk

Third edition 2003

British Library Cataloguing in Publication Data
A catalogue record for this book is available from
the British Library.

Produced for How To Books by Deer Park Productions
Typeset by Anneset, Weston-super-Mare, North Somerset
Cover design by Baseline Arts Ltd, Oxford
Printed and bound by Cromwell Press, Trowbridge, Wiltshire

Contents

List of Illustrations

Preface
to the third edition

Italy, particularly the central regions of Tuscany, Umbria and Marche, has a growing expatriate population. The Italian lifestyle, the wealth of culture and the excellent food attract more people every year, whether it is to start a new life or to take an extended holiday. Those travelling with children will appreciate just how much Italians love *bambini*, while any foreigner is generally made to feel welcome as Italians are immensely proud of their country and enjoy sharing it with visitors.

Going to Live in Italy aims to help visitors experience the real Italy and is ideal for those who want to venture off the beaten track and do things the Italian way. When in Rome do as the Romans do . . . is just what this book is about, helping you in various situations ranging from driving a car to buying a house. This book will probably make you more Italian than the average Italian and take out some of the headaches that being *stranieri* can present. Have a great stay in Italy and good luck!

Amanda Hinton

1

Italy in Brief

INTRODUCING THE COUNTRY

The 'boot' that makes up mainland Italy has its toe in the Mediterranean, the Adriatic on its eastern flank and the Tyrrhenian on the west. The coast, including the islands of Sardinia and Sicily, is 7,420 km long; mountains make up 35.2 per cent of the country, while gently folding hills cover just over 40 per cent of the rest. All of this makes for a very scenic country, with each region having its own character and landscape.

For purposes of administration Italy is divided into 20 regions: Piedmont, Aosta, Lombardy, Trentino-Alto Adige, Veneto, Friuli-Venezia Giulia, Liguria, Emilia Romagna, Tuscany, Umbria, Marche, Lazio, Abruzzo, Molise, Puglia, Campania, Basilicata, Calabria, Sicily and Sardinia. The regions are further subdivided, and comprise 95 provinces with over 8,000 municipalities, each of which has a strong sense of identity thanks to the Italians' inherent *campanilismo*, parochialism, and sense of local pride.

Pride in all things Italian and a love of life have been little dampened by the continuing economic recession, and Italy continues to be one of the biggest markets for French champagne, Scotch whisky and Rolls Royce cars. Many Italians spend their summer holidays in exotic destinations as well as taking a *settimana bianca* ski holiday during the winter. The close-knit structure of the family helps finance these luxuries as old-age pensions are pooled into the household fund.

ITALIAN-STYLE ECONOMICS

In 1992, Italy had the largest budget deficit in the world, amounting to 11 per cent of its total economic output. However, by raising VAT rates and exercising stringent budget controls, Italy accomplished the feat of meeting European Union requirements for entry into European Monetary Union in 1997. In the following years, the growth rate in the Italian economy excelled most other European countries. In fact, the statistics are misleading regarding general national wealth due to the continuing huge disparity between the industrial north and the struggling south. In 2001, the growth rate began a serious slowdown due to an increase in public spending and the looming future budget deficit is likely to be too hefty to meet the European guidelines. The remnant 'hidden economy' also has to be taken into account. A great many companies are not legally registered and a large proportion of the labour market is unregulated. For example, Naples is a centre for the production of gloves, yet there is hardly a single registered glove-making company in the city.

Perhaps the greatest drain on the Italian economy has been the mismanagement of funds, with huge sums of money being poured into public construction projects that are rarely completed. The vast and empty aqueducts crossing the parched countryside in the southern regions of Reggio Calabria, and the non-existent housing for earthquake victims, are some of the more poignant examples of funds being intercepted. It's a depressingly commonplace scenario, with

Fig.1. Map of Italy.

fortunes being taken from the industrial north to improve the south, but ending up in the pockets of everyone except the people who need it. At the same time, there has been an added strain on State funds as a result of the earthquakes in 1998 causing endless damage to buildings, including public monuments such as the Basilica at Assisi in Central Italy.

POLITICAL LIFE

Like the economy, the government is also in a state of tumult. For almost 50 years the same people, entrenched in cold-war politics, had been in power, albeit in changed seats. In April 1992, however, the veteran Prime Minister, Giulio Andreotti, who was known for his *immobilismo*, was superceded by Giuliano Amato. Amongst other radical changes, Amato was responsible for introducing an austerity budget in order to bring inflation down to European levels, making sweeping reforms of the welfare state and abolishing the *scala mobili*, the inflationary wage indexation system.

Since 1992, there have been several prime ministers including Massimo d'Alema who was elected in October 1998. The 1994 elections voted in Silvio Berlusconi; however, he was forced to step down in 1995 when a member of his coalition party withdrew support. The Berlusconi government was succeeded by a technical government headed by Prime Minister Lamberto Dini which fell in early 1996. In April 1996, national elections were held again and led to the victory of a centre left coalition (The Olive Tree), led by Romano Prodi. In the April 1997 local elections, voters split almost evenly between centre right and centre left coalitions before the election of d'Alema in 1998.

The 1990s also saw the challenging appearance of *leghe*, regional independence movements. At the same time the 1990s heralded the exposure of Italy's institutional crime. Hundreds of politicians and businessmen were arrested for raking off funds into party or personal coffers and billions of dollars of public money were lost in *tangenti*, kick-backs to secure public contracts. New electoral systems, and a sweeping out of the old faces, coupled with a strengthening of the controls over public funds, look like doing much to overcome this crisis.

Another dramatic turn of the 1990s was in connection with the Mafia. The savage assassination of the top anti-Mafia investigators, Judge Falcone and his successor Judge Borsellino, sparked a popular revolt in the summer of 1992. For the first time people had the courage to voice opinions that they formerly would not even have dared to think. The Mafia will only be swept away when an honest government once again exerts control, and when the law of silence, the *omertá*, is finally broken. For a country which normally changes its prime minister every nine months, the continuity of the term of office of Silvio Berlusconi, elected in 2001 after the victory of his centre right bloc coalition, promises a more stable and realistic economy. Berlusconi pledged 'a new era' for Italians, proclaiming 'I am convinced that you all feel the need for a government that governs and of a premier who speaks less and works more and better'.

2

Before You Go

PREPARING PAPERWORK

UK visitors need the bare minimum of documents to enter Italy. However, Italian bureaucracy with its kilometres of red tape has a way of multiplying the papers needed in any operation, so that in reality you will find that the more documents you can take with you, the better. Obtaining the necessary documents from the UK before travelling to Italy is a wise move, especially if you are intending to become a permanent resident in Italy. If you are making a long-term move try to allow about three months in order to make a thorough job of preparing your papers and tying up all the loose ends before your departure.

Passports and visas

To visit Italy a valid passport, or in the case of EU citizens an identity card, is all that is necessary. British citizens who wish to stay in Italy for more than three months should have a standard ten-year passport rather than the temporary visitor's passport.

Non-EU citizens can stay for up to 90 days. However, visa requirements for citizens of individual countries should be checked at an Italian Consulate (see Appendix for addresses). Should you need a visa you will have to submit an application form and one passport-sized photograph.

EU citizens are permitted an unlimited stay without requiring the *permesso di soggiorno* that was necessary in the past.

Other documents

If you intend to register for work in Italy you will need authenticated translations made of your educational or professional qualifications, as well as certificates of equivalence. British nationals requiring a European Community Certificate of Experience, which Italy is required to recognise as a substitute for the relevant national qualification, can obtain guidance packs and application forms from the Department of Trade and Industry (DTI) at the following address:

Certificates of Experience Unit
Department of Trade and Industry
2nd Floor
Kingsgate House
66–74 Victoria Street
London SW1E 6SW
Tel: 020 7215 4004

If you are self-employed and intend to continue in self-employment in Italy, you must also apply to the DTI for a European Community Certificate of Experience. The certificate is only awarded if you have gained the necessary experience and qualifications in your particular area of work. Contact the DTI at the above address and ask for form EC2 which is completed with an application fee of £105. The DTI also provide information on the comparability of professional and academic qualifications in the free booklet *Europe Open for Professions*.

Academic and scholastic certificates of equivalence, known as *Certificato di Equipollenza*, are undertaken by:

Presidenza Consiglio Ministri
Ministerio Coordinamento Politiche Comunitarie
Via Giardino Theodoli 66
00186 Roma
Tel: 06 67791/67795322

Ufficio VI
Equipollenze per i paesi Anglofoni
Direzione Generale per le Relazioni Culturali
Ministero degli Affari Esteri
Piazzale Della Farnesina,
00194 Roma
Tel: 06 326489

Guidance about vocational qualifications in the UK can be obtained from:

The Public Enquiry Unit
DfES
Lower Ground Floor
Sanctuary Buildings
Great Smith Street
London SW1P 3BT
Tel: 0870 0002288

Further information on academic recognition can be obtained from the following addresses:

Carlo Finocchietti
Centro Informazione sulla Mobilità e le Equivalenze
Accademiche (CIMEA)

Fondazione RUI
Viale Ventuno Aprile
36-00162 Roma
Tel: 06 86321281

Italian Consulate, or the British Council, or the Department of Trade and Industry (see Appendix of Further Information for addresses).

For some general guidelines consult *The International Guide to Qualifications in Education*, 4th edition 1996, published by Mansell plc. This publication contains an evaluation in terms of British qualifications for the main academic qualifications awarded overseas. It can generally be found in main reference libraries.

If you are not going to work, but intend to live on savings while in Italy, you should obtain a letter from your bank stating your financial position.

If you are moving to Italy with your children you should also have authenticated translations made of any educational and vaccination documents they have. To obtain authenticated translations and certificates, contact your nearest Italian Consulate well in advance of leaving (see Appendix for Consulate addresses). The pre-school immunisation programme in Italy differs slightly from that in the UK. It is advisable to be as up to date as possible with your child's immunisation programme before leaving the UK.

Arranging travel insurance

If you intend to take out travel insurance it is best to select a comprehensive policy. This should include medical expenses, personal accident insurance, flight cancellation, personal liability as well as covering personal effects. Remember that if you need to make a claim you will be requested to supply receipts. As this is not always possible, it may be a good idea to have older items, such as jewellery, individually valued and recorded. Keeping a photographic record is not such a bad idea as it offers the insurance company some idea of the objects being claimed for, as well as some proof of their existence.

Health insurance

British citizens, or nationals of other European Union countries who are resident in the UK, are entitled to subsidised medical care under the **Italian State Health Service.** In order to apply, go to a main post office or a social security office and ask for leaflet T6 *Health Advice for Travellers* which has a blank E111 in the back. The E111 is your certificate of entitlement and should be presented when medical care is needed, along with proof of your UK residence. It is advisable to take your NHS card for this purpose, although a passport or driving licence will suffice. You may also be asked to provide a photocopy of your E111, so have a spare copy handy.

It may be worth considering a private health insurance policy which would enable you to opt out of the Italian State Health system, as this only provides emergency treatment, doctors and paediatricians free of charge. You will also find that in major cities and in the south of Italy, the State Health system is often overstretched and sub-standard.

- Note that you are only eligible for an E111 if you continue to be a resident of the UK and maintain your National Insurance contributions. Therefore make sure that the DSS Overseas Department (see Appendix for address) is informed of the state of your National Insurance contributions before leaving Britain. You should also remember that an E111 is only valid for one year.

Anyone intending to take up residency in Italy must join the Italian health service (see Chapter 6) or take out a private health insurance policy. Once you start paying contributions to the Italian system, you are eligible for Italian State Healthcare.

Immunisation

No vaccinations are required to enter Italy.

Social Security

Are you unemployed? Have you been receiving Job Seekers' Allowance in Britain for at least four weeks and intend looking for work in Italy? If so you may have your payments transferred for up to three months from the day on which you leave the UK. If you are looking for work let the Job Centre know well in advance of leaving the country and ask for form E303, from the post office which is a transfer of entitlement to look for work in Italy. You should also ask the Job Centre for an introductory letter which is written in Italian (known as DLJA403) by the Benefits Agency. This will help you when you register for employment in Italy. If you are registered at a Job Centre in the UK, ask to be registered as a Job Seeker in Italy. Your details will then be forwarded to the Italian Employment Office *(Ufficio Collocamento)*. Another useful leaflet available from Job Centres, JSAL22, explains what happens when you go overseas to look for work.

Note that once you have received contribution-based Job Seekers' Allowance in Italy, you cannot receive it again for another length of time when you are seeking work abroad unless you have done more work and paid into the UK National Insurance scheme.

If you are receiving Sickness Benefit or Maternity Allowance you should be able to receive payments in Italy until it expires. However, write well in advance to the Department of Social Security Overseas Branch (see Appendix for address) and ask for their authorisation.

If you are receiving a UK Retirement Pension you will continue to receive your payments in Italy. Payments are made either directly by postal orders, or can be deposited in a UK or Italian bank account or building society. Make sure you arrange exactly how the payments are to be paid before leaving.

For further information obtain the DSS pamphlet SA29, *Your Social Security and Pension Rights in the European Community,* and pamphlet NI 38 or tel: 0191 2187652 for further information.

Students

Students planning to attend an Italian university must go to an Italian Consulate before leaving and obtain a certified declaration stating their acceptance on a course. Students should also make sure that they obtain form E111 (see health insurance above). For further information on applying for a place at an Italian university see Chapter 8.

Students should also remember to take their student identity card in order to receive discounts on museum entrance fees and travel.

Liability to British tax

Careful consideration needs to be given to the benefits and disadvantages of being either a British or an Italian tax payer, or both. The tax laws are numerous and complex in both countries, and constantly change, and it is a good idea to seek professional help on this matter.

However, some general principles are useful to bear in mind. First, Italy and Britain have a **double-taxation agreement** which means that the same income is never taxed in both countries, and that the two tax authorities come to an agreement about who taxes what according to:

- where your principal residence is
- where your income is generated
- and what your nationality is.

Secondly, that exemption from British tax is granted if you are deemed non-resident. To qualify for that status you need to work overseas full time for a year, visit the UK for less than three months a year, have no available accommodation there, nor perform any part of your job there. The exception to this rule is income that derives from property rented out in the UK, which is always liable for UK taxation. If you are planning a short-term stay in Italy you will therefore remain liable to UK income tax, and probably only come up against Italian taxes if you own a property in Italy.

The first step in declaring non-resident status is to read leaflet IR20 which explains liability to tax in the UK as a resident or non-resident and to request Form P85 from your local tax or PAYE office which should be issued with leaflet IR138, *Living or Retiring Abroad*. Form P85 informs the Inland Revenue that you are leaving the UK as well as prompting any tax refund that may be due from previous employment. Whether you are eligible for non-resident status or not ordinarily resident status is a matter that is ultimately decided by the International Division of the Inland Revenue. For queries concerning non-residency, the Division can be contacted at the following address:

Inland Revenue FICO
Residence Advice and Liabilities Section
Room 220
St John's House
Merton Road
Bootle
Merseyside L69 9BB
Tel: 0151 472 6284
www.inlandrevenue.gov.uk

The International Division also issues self assessment forms in which it is possible to declare your own residential status as well as forms for split year claims when you are a UK resident for only part of any one tax year.

Banking

If you are claiming non-resident status in Britain you should inform your bank or building society so that you are exempted from paying tax on any interest that you accrue. You may wish to arrange offshore banking; most of the national banks have offshore branches, which means you can simply transfer your account from one branch to another. It is a good idea to keep a sterling account open as Italian banking is expensive and does not offer the same customer services or facilities. Make sure, however, that you have good access to your sterling account, preferably with an international card that can be used in automatic banking machines at principal Italian banks.

Driving documents

Drivers in Italy will need a current driving licence. If you have a pre-1996 green-style UK driving licence, you will need to apply for an International Driving Permit. Available online at www.theaa.com, the permit costs £4 and is valid for 12 months. Drivers with the EEC-format licences, which are pink, or more recently, pink and green, do not need to carry a translation.

Other documents you should have include:

- **green card insurance**, if Italy is not covered on your regular insurance policy
- **V5 Registration Document** (log book)
- a **GB sticker**, on display.

British-plate vehicles

In European countries you are allowed to drive a foreign vehicle for 12 months. In Italy, however, British-registered vehicles can only be driven with their original plates for up to six months in any one 12-month period. Italy also bucks the European norm on importation laws, which is obligatory after six months. It is extraordinarily difficult to import vehicles, and the authorities may well advise you to continue driving on your original plates and rely on the police turning a blind eye. As the procedure for importing a vehicle is painstakingly long, you should consider very carefully whether you really need to import your car into Italy, or whether it would be better to sell it in the UK before departure and purchase another upon arrival in Italy, even if car prices are somewhat higher there.

If you are certain you wish to import your vehicle, then apply for leaflet V526 from a Vehicle Registration Office or from:

DVLA
Swansea
SA99 1BL or go to www.dvla.gov.uk

The leaflet tells the procedure for exporting vehicles. Before leaving Britain complete your V5 Registration Document and return it to Swansea or your regional Vehicle Registration Office, stating the date on which you intend to export the vehicle. You should also request that your V5 Registration Document, or an authenticated photocopy, is returned along with a **Certificate of Export V561.** Italy is unusual in that it requests the V5 as well as the V561; normally the V561 replaces the V5. Once in possession of both these documents you should have them translated into Italian and authenticated. The Italian authorities also request a **Scheda Tecnica** which is technical data concerning your vehicle. This should be available from the head office of the manufacturers of your vehicle. Again this needs to be translated and authenticated. Finally get a copy of the vehicle sales invoice showing the amount of VAT paid. You may be requested to pay the difference between UK and Italian VAT when you cross the border into Italy. The next stage in the formalities takes place in Italy (see Chapter 4).

Tips on car importing
Here are some tips if you are trying to import your vehicle into Italy.

- Cars made outside the EU are almost impossible to import and invoke the payment of very high import taxes.

- To avoid the payment of customs duty and import tax the owner must have owned the vehicle for at least 12 months prior to the date of importation.

- Make sure your V561 certificate of export is stamped when crossing the border into Italy, as this will be proof of the actual date on which you officially imported the vehicle.

- For ease of servicing and parts Renault, Fiat, Volkswagen, Audi, Alfa-Romeo and Mercedes are the most common cars in Italy.

Pets

If you are travelling with a domestic animal you will be asked to present a bilingual **Export Health Certificate** and a **Rabies Certificate** when you enter Italy. To obtain these certificates apply to your local vet or to DEFRA (Department for Environment and Rural Affairs) at the address below and request application form EXA1.

DEFRA
1a Page Street
London SW1P 4PQ
Tel: 020 7904 6000

On receipt of application form EXA1, fill in the necessary information and send it to your local Animal Health Office, which will issue the certificate to an approved Local Veterinary Inspector. The Inspector is responsible for completing the export certificate and examining your animal within 48 hours of your departure.

The rabies vaccine will also be administered by the Local Veterinary Inspector, who will attach the Rabies Certificate to the Export Health Certificate. The rabies vaccine should be given not less than 20 days and not more than 11 months before leaving the UK.

Animals under three months of age, and animals who are being transported unaccompanied, are exempt from the rabies vaccine, although they must undergo an examination by an Italian Veterinary Officer when entering Italy.

If you are travelling through other places on the way to Italy, apply to the authorities in the relevant countries.

CHECKLIST OF DOCUMENTS

Make sure you have the following:

Passport or Identity Card   _____

Form E111 and/or health insurance   _____

NHS card   _____

Travel insurance policy   _____

Student Identity Card   _____

Export Health Certificate (for pets) _____

Rabies Vaccination Certificate (for pets) _____

Driving Licence _____

Translation of Driving Licence _____

Green card insurance _____

V5 Registration Document _____

V561 Certificate of Export _____

Vehicle sales invoice _____

WHAT ARE YOU TAKING?

Those planning a short visit to Italy will probably find that everything they require is available there, and need only concern themselves with the customs regulations. Those planning a longer-term trip, or to take up residence in Italy, will find this section helpful as it also suggests what might be taken out to Italy, either because it is not readily available, or because it is considerably more expensive there.

Customs allowances

Duty free alcohol and cigarettes are no longer available for EU countries. In theory, there are no longer any restrictions on the quantities you can buy, as long as they are for private consumption. However, individual countries in the EU issue specific guidelines. If you are travelling from the UK to Italy, these are:

- 60 ml perfume
- 250 ml eau de toilette
- 200 cigarettes
- 2 litres still table wine
- 1 litre of spirits
- other goods for personal use, up to the value of approx. £60.

If you are travelling from Italy to the UK, the guidelines are the same, with one exception

- 50 ml perfume.

The restrictions on personal effects are supposedly lifted for EU citizens. However, in reality you may be faced with problems when it comes to items such as electrical appliances. If you are moving from Britain to Italy you are likewise free to move your household belongings and personal effects, provided that you have owned them for more than three months and that you paid tax on purchasing them. The only way of proving this is with a sales invoice, so before you leave gather together as many invoices as possible for items you intend to take. If you plan to move your household belongings in stages you will still be exempt from paying tax, provided they are moved within six months of the date you acquired residence in Italy. Exemption from taxes also applies to those moving household effects from Britain to a holiday home in Italy, provided you are the owner of the property or have been paying rent for at least 12 months.

Money

The Euro replaced the much-loved lira as the legal currency of Italy on 1 January 2002.

- Notes are issued for 5, 10, 20, 50, 100, 200 and 500 Euros.

One Euro is divided into one hundred cents and the eight denominations of coins vary in colour and thickness according to their values.

- Coins are of denominations 1, 2, 5, 10, 20 and 50 cents.

The Euro quickly gained in strength against the pound sterling and, although fluctuating daily, is taken here as approximately 1.55 Euros to the pound sterling.

Furnishings

If you are setting up a home in Italy it is worth considering transporting your furniture from Britain, as it is considerably more expensive in Italy and the cost of replacing household furniture is likely to be higher than the cost of using an international removal firm. There are few secondhand furniture shops in Italy, and old furniture such as pine cupboards and chests of drawers are regarded as antiques and fetch exorbitant prices by British standards.

If you are bringing furniture over 50 years old from Britain you should apply for permission from the Italian Ministry of Culture beforehand, and then declare it on arrival, to avoid difficulties in re-exporting it. The address for the Italian Ministry of Culture is:

Ministerio per i Beni e le Attività Culturali
Via Baudana Vaccolini Costanza 6
00153 Roma
Tel: 06 5810846.

If you are planning to decorate your home in Italy you will find DIY materials cheaper and more readily available in Britain. This is especially true of paint, both emulsion and gloss, which are of a far higher quality in the UK, and lower prices. It is worth noting that DIY, known as *fai da te*, is in its infancy in Italy. Very few people do their own work, and DIY kits such as flat-pack units or self-assembly articles like roller blinds are not generally available. As Italians take their kitchens with them when they move house you are more than likely to have to put in a new one when buying a property. Great savings can be made by bringing out a complete flat-pack kitchen from the UK, as Italian kitchens, while very attractive, are also very expensive.

Floor coverings are also something you may wish to consider bringing from Britain. Italian homes generally have tiled floors; fitted carpets are not very common and you pay a lot for what seems, by comparison to UK standards, poor quality carpeting.

Bedding in Italy consists mainly of blankets and eiderdowns. If you prefer to sleep under a duvet it is a good thing to bring, as although they are available in some places they are very much more expensive than in the UK.

Electrical appliances

Electrical appliances in Italy run on 220v. In general, it is slightly more expensive to buy electrical appliances in Italy, but on the whole it is more convenient as they are covered by local guarantee and can be repaired easily. Something you are well advised to bring with you, however, is an electric kettle, as they are hard to come by and very expensive in Italy.

If you are bringing electrical appliances from Britain bring the sales invoice as proof that you have paid VAT. As VAT is higher in Italy, you may be requested to pay the difference between the two rates when you cross the border. Televisions and music centres tend to cause problems at customs and duty may have to be paid. It should also be noted that British TV sets do not generally function satisfactorily in Italy. The same is true for UK portable telephones.

Do not bring lamps or lights with bayonet fittings, unless you are also prepared to bring a good supply of light bulbs with you, as only the screw-in type are sold in Italy. If you are bringing appliances with a built-in plug you will need an adaptor, as Italian plugs have two or three pins in a row.

Clothing and shoes

Italians live up to their reputation for chic fashion, and dress with great care and expense. The *passeggiata*, the evening stroll that most Italians take along a town's main *corso*, is an important social ritual. Appearance is everything and design-er labels score the highest marks. It is rare to see an Italian in a pair of patched jeans or an old jumper — unless of course it is part of a fashion statement. Casual dressing simply does not happen very much. By comparison most British visitors seem disastrously underdressed and shabby.

If you have a limited budget you should bring as much cloth-ing with you as possible, for other than outdoor markets there are few places to buy cut-price clothing. Sales, *saldi*, take place in January and early February, and also in late July and August before summer vacation begins. But even if there is a 50 per cent discount on a sweater that was £150 it still seems quite expensive by British high street standards. For a winter stay include a raincoat and a winter coat in your packing as winters can be surprisingly cold. If you have a fur coat this may be your best chance to wear it. Animal rights campaigners are not very active in Italy and few Italians have any compunction about wearing fur.

Sportswear is also something you should consider bringing with you as it, and sports equipment, is generally more expensive in Italy.

If you like to make your own clothes you may wish to bring paper patterns with you. The selection in Italy is restricted to Burda patterns and you may find the instructions stretch your Italian to its limit.

Babycare and children's clothing

The cost of clothing, toys, baby foods and babycare items is considerably higher in Italy than in the UK. You will find no equivalent to Mothercare, Boots, Early Learning or any other of the reasonably-priced chain stores that exist in Britain. Prenatal, one of the biggest children's chains in Italy, has a full range of products, but prices are high. Therefore bring as much as possible with you, especially if there is food your child particularly enjoys. The selection of baby food is somewhat restricted and the Italian diet is very different to the British.

Food

Italians take immense pride and pleasure in their national cuisine, and ingredients for other cuisines are not widely available, so such things as spices and condiments should be brought with you. Cooking utensils such as woks and lidded saucepans with single handles are also not very commonplace.

Imported tea is available but is sold in small quantities at twice the UK price. Baking powder and icing sugar are also sold in very small quantities. Food colouring and many flavourings are not commonly available in Italy as they have been withdrawn for health reasons.

Books and stationery

A good supply of general reading material is a must, for unless you are in a large city or a town with a high student population you will find English books hard to come by. In the major cities there are of course bookshops which carry reasonable selections of English literature and in Rome there is a second-hand English book shop near the Opera.

Most stationery items are readily available, with the exception of Blu-Tac. All computer services are also easily found, including those for Amstrad, Phillips and Apple.

Pharmaceuticals and toiletries

If you take a regular prescribed drug bring a good supply in order to give you time to locate its equivalent in Italy. Many drugs are marketed under different names. Your doctor or the drug manufacturer should be able to tell you the brand name used in Italy, and whether the formula given in Italy is exactly the same as your current prescription.

The Bodyshop has branches in the major cities throughout Italy. However, there is no real equivalent to Boots, and there are few toiletries for the middle of the market. Most are sold in small boutiques which specialise in designer brands, or in supermarkets alongside the bleach and the toothbrushes. The same applies to cosmetics. Face flannels are not used by Italians and are not easily available.

CHECKLIST OF ITEMS NOT READILY AVAILABLE IN ITALY

- wall-to-wall floor coverings
- window blinds
- secondhand furniture
- electric kettles
- woks
- lidded saucepans with a single handle
- oriental foods and spices
- reading material
- Blu-Tac
- face flannels.

GETTING TO ITALY

By air

The fastest and in many cases the most economical way to travel to Italy is by air, its only real disadvantage being that luggage allowances are minimal. For this reason those setting up a holiday home will probably be wise to travel and transport their goods and chattels by car, perhaps in a number of stages. However, those setting up a permanent home might find the combination of an overland removals firm for the household goods and a cheap flight the best solution, as it avoids the problem of having to convert a UK-registered car into an Italian one. The normal baggage allowance on flights is 20kg per person, or 30kg if you are travelling first class, with excess baggage charged per kilo at first class travel rates.

The cost of air flights to Italy varies greatly, depending on the type of flight and ticket you book.

The Internet has changed air travel in more than one way, affecting the way in which flights are booked and placing increasing pressure on prices. It is rather like the stock exchange, prices leap up and down so that the best option is to shop around for flights. When booking flights, you might need to check the flexibility. Some flights stipulate a minimum or maximum length of stay and cannot be changed or modified. Most airlines offer discounts for travellers aged between 12 and 26 while some can offer discounted car hire packages with flight. The journey from London to Rome takes two and a quarter hours and to Milan it takes just under two hours. Airlines operating between the UK and Italy have websites which are useful for looking up bargain fares; alternatively bookings can be made over the phone or through a tour operator.

Alitalia: www.alitalia.it Tel: 0870 544 8259.
Go Fly: www.go-fly.com Tel: 0870 607 6543.
KLM UK: www.klmuk.com Tel: 08705 074074.
Ryan Air: www.ryanair.com Tel: 0871 246 0000.
Virgin Express: www.virgin-express.com
   Tel: 020 7744 0004.

Italian airports

The principal Italian airports with regular scheduled and charter flights from Britain are as follows:

Alghero	Fertilia Airport
Bari	Palese Airport
Bologna	Guglielmo Marconi Airport
Brindisi	Perozzi Airport
Cagliari	Mario Mameli Airport
Catania	Fontanarossa Airport
Florence	Peretola Airport
Genoa	C. Colombo Airport
Milan	Linate and Malpensa Airports
Naples	Capodichino Airport
Palermo	Punta Raisi Airport
Perugia	S.Egidio
Pisa	Galileo Galilei Airport
Rome	Leonardo da Vinci and Ciampino Fiumincino Airports
Turin	Caselle Airport
Venice	Marco Polo Tessera Airport

UK charter flights also make use of the following airports, although many are in operation during the summer season only:

Ancona	Falconara Raffaello Sanzio Airport
Bergamo	Orio al Serio Airport
Brindisi	Perozzi Airport
Lamezia Terme	Santa Eufemia Airport
Olbia	Costa Smeralda Airport
Pescara	Saga Aeroporto D'ambruzzo Airport

Rimini	Miramare Airport
Treviso	San Giuseppe Airport
Trieste	Ronchi del Legionari Airport
Verona	Valerio Catullo/Villafranca Airport

Flights from the USA

Those travelling from the USA may be able to use their Frequent Flyer Program. Otherwise a standard APEX return from New York to Rome costs approximately $900. Charter fares may be slightly lower; details can be found at your local travel agent or by scanning the adverts in the Sunday travel supplements. Airlines flying regularly from New York to Italy include Alitalia, Lufthansa and United Airlines:

Alitalia
666 Fifth Avenue
New York NY 10103
Tel: (212) 903 3300

United Airlines
605 Third Avenue
New York NY 10016
Tel: (212) 290 2141
www.ual.com

Going by car

The journey from London to Rome is a somewhat gruelling 1,800km, which normally involves about 20 hours of driving. It is best spread over two days as the quickest route, on the motorways, is really monotonous. Unless you are sharing the cost between four passengers, travelling by car is more expensive than flying, as on top of the basic fuel cost there is also the cross-channel ferry or train to pay for, motorway tolls in both France and Italy, as well as accommodation and other general travel expenses. The most direct and quickest route is by taking the Euro Tunnel (eurotunnel.com) or the short ferry crossing from Dover or Folkestone to Calais or Boulogne, then driving through France to Basel in Switzerland. P & O Stena Line (www.posl.com) operates regular crossings from Dover to Calais and offers plenty to do for children and adults en route with a range of shops and activity areas. For information or reservations call 0870 6000600 – remember to check out bargain crossings, if you intend to use this ferry route on a regular basis. At the Swiss border you will be requested to pay a tax which is levied on all Swiss road users and be presented with a sticker to display in your window, which permits you to use the Swiss road system until the end of the year in which it is issued. Finally, from Switzerland head through the Alps via the Gotthard Tunnel to Milan. Otherwise you can avoid Switzerland by crossing the Alps via the Mont Blanc tunnel. An alternative route is to take the longer ferry crossing to Ostend or Zeebrugge, and travel through Belgium and Germany where the motorways are free, although you will have to pay for the Brenner Autobahn in Austria.

By coach

The cost and time entailed in travelling to Italy by coach again make flying the more desirable option. A return ticket from London to Rome comes to around £111 and the journey from London to Turin, which is one of the closest destinations in Italy, takes approximately 22 hours. From London Victoria Coach Station the route passes via Dover, Paris, Mont Blanc and Aosta, from where the itinerary depends on your destination. Major destinations include Turin, Genoa,

Milan, Venice, Bologna, Florence and Rome. For further details contact any National Express office in the UK or one of the addresses below:

National Express Ltd
PO Box 9854
Birmingham
B16 8XN
Tel: 08705 808080

Eurolines UK Ltd
4 Cardiff Road
Luton
LU1 1PP
Tel: 08705 143219
or book online at www.gobycoach.com

Going by train

Travelling by rail from Britain to Italy has the advantage of giving you the opportunity to stop by at other destinations in Europe. Tickets issued in Britain are valid for up to two months and have no restrictions on the number of times you break your journey. If you intend to meander your way to Italy you will find the *Thomas Cook European Timetable* invaluable. It is published monthly, so make sure you get an up to date version, and is available from any Thomas Cook branch or by post from:

Thomas Cook Timetable Publishing
PO Box 227, The Thomas Cook Business Park
Peterborough PE3 8XX
Tel: 01733 416477
or order online from www.thomascookpublishing.com

If you purchase an inter-rail card, available for young people up to 26 years old, you will be given a 50 per cent discount on railways in Italy until its expiry date. The under 26s can also obtain discounts with a BIJE card. This is a personal international second class ticket, valid for two months, which entitles the holder to a discount on a chosen route. The discount varies according to the railway network used, but is generally 30 per cent. The card is available from tour operators and Transalpino, Wasteels and Eurotrain/CTS.

Senior Citizen cards are also valid in Italy and give you considerable reductions.

A normal return ticket from London to Rome costs in the region of £200. You can expect to pay a supplement on top of this for a sleeping berth. A direct trip from London to Rome takes about 26 hours, the four commonest routes from London being as follows:

- London, Calais, Paris, Modena, Turin
- London, Calais, Switzerland, Chiassio, Milan
- London, Calais, Paris, French Riviera, Ventimiglia
- London, Ostend, Karlsruhe, Munich, Brenner.

The Orient Express
If you want to arrive in Italy in style there is always the Orient Express which runs from London to Venice via Paris and Milan. You can expect to pay from £1235 upwards for a single journey, inclusive of meals. For further details contact www.orient-expresstrains.com

Italian State Railway
Tickets can be booked online for the Italian State Railway at www.trenitalia.com with secure credit card facility and received at your home address or collected from self service machines at main railway stations.

Removals

If you are moving your household belongings from Britain to Italy you will probably be using an international removal firm. You are well advised to use one that takes responsibility for all the paperwork involved, which includes writing a full inventory in both English and Italian. Most removal firms also take charge of the packing and unpacking. The cost of the removal depends on the volume of your belongings. A full container load might cost around £2,500. However, if two or three households share a container you can save up to £600. The problem with sharing a container is waiting for other households in the same area. The most frequent removals are made to Northern Italy during the summer. Below are the addresses of some of the international removal companies in Britain. Other companies can be found by simply looking in the *Yellow Pages*.

Allied Pickfords
Heritage House
345 Southbury Road
Enfield
Middlesex EN1 1UP
Tel: 0800 289 229
www.pickfords.co.uk

Crown Worldwide Movers
Kingsbridge Road
Barking
Essex IG11 0BD
Tel: 020 8591 3388
www.crownworldwide.com

Martell's International Removers
Queen's Road
East Grinstead
West Sussex
RH19 1BA
Tel: 01342 321303
www.martells.co.uk

CASE HISTORY: ARRIVING BY CAMPERVAN

Malcolm and Sandra came to Italy with a campervan, with the intention of buying a property, but before leaving the UK they failed to execute the necessary formalities, the V5, the V561 and the *scheda tecnica*. After purchasing their property they discovered exactly what was required and had to return to the UK to obtain the necessary documents. So far so good, even if the trip home was an unnecessary expense. They decided to apply for the *scheda tecnica* in Italy and managed to obtain it from the manufacturer, only to discover that their camper was classified as a van. The authorities in Italy didn't recognise the vehicle as being the same as that in the documents in which it was described as a camper. The result was that they were forced either to reimport it back to the UK (which was difficult as the exportation was never properly completed) or to drive it illegally in Italy and risk its confiscation and a hefty fine.

Advice: buy in Italy and don't attempt to import; or get your paperwork right at the very start.

3

Getting Around

TRANSPORT

The public transport system in Italy is well used and reasonably priced by European standards, but it is chaotic at the best of times. Probably the most efficient services are run by private transport companies which operate on a small local scale in towns and around their outlying villages. The railway system, which is for the most part state owned, suffers in the same way that most public services do in Italy. It seems to exist entirely for its own benefit, is inefficient and out of date. The ticket system is complicated, the trains are notoriously unpunctual and for a few days every so often the system is paralysed by strikes. Travelling by ferry, either between the mainland and Italian islands, or on internal waters, is both pleasant and fairly well organised. Those short of time can also take advantage of the extensive domestic airways network which operates regular flights between the major Italian cities.

Travelling by railway

The boot of Italy is almost completely girdled by railway tracks. This does little to enhance the coastline, but it makes for scenic train rides and preserves Italy's mountainous interior. The great majority of the network, which covers some 19,588km and has around 3,500 stations, is owned by the state and is known as the *Ferrovie Statale*. There are however a few private lines, such as that which rings Mount Vesuvius in Southern Italy.

The fares for travelling by train are calculated according to distance travelled, the type of train, and whether you choose a first or second class seat. Below is a list of the various types of trains, arranged in order of cost and speed at which they travel.

- ETR 450 Pendolino
- Eurostar Italia (TAV)
- Express
- Diretto
- Locale

The ETR 450, 460 and 480 Pendolino is a first class, high speed train for which reservations are obligatory. Running between Milan and Rome, the train is designed to compete with air services. The latest ETR 500 reaches a speed of 300 km per hour. Seat reservation is also obligatory on Eurostar Italia trains. A *rapido* supplement of around 30 per cent of the cost of the fare is levied on most lines. With the introduction of the ETR 480 and 500, the old ETR trains are being converted to sleepers. The principal routes covered by these night trains connect Puglia with Milan and Rome.

The Express and Diretto also cover long distances but stop frequently, particularly the Diretto. The Locale only runs short distances and dawdles interminably at each station, as it usually has to give way to any train of a higher category and is frequently overtaken.

Seat reservations can be made from two months up to three hours before the time of departure, bookings being taken at the railway station or from an authorised travel agency. When you board the train you will find your seat is reserved with a card bearing your name. However, once the train has started reserved seats that are not occupied may be taken by other passengers. If you buy your ticket on the train you will have to pay a surcharge of 20 per cent.

Rail cards and economy tickets
Before booking a ticket you may wish to look into the various types of rail cards and economy tickets that exist.

- **Carta Verde** is a youth rail card for people aged between 12 and 26 years. It offers a discount of 20 per cent for one year on the fare for first and second class tickets. Those travelling to Greece by railway may also use the *Carta Verde* to obtain a 50 per cent discount on specified ferry crossings. The card costs 26 Euros.

- **Carta d'Argento** is a personal seasonal ticket, valid for one year, which allows people over 60 years to purchase first and second class tickets with a 20 per cent discount on basic fares on all national routes. The card costs 26 Euros.

- If you are not a resident of Italy you can purchase the **Italy Rail Card**. This ticket gives unlimited travel on the State railway network for a period of 8, 15, 21 or 30 days, depending on the length of time you wish. You can travel in first or second class, there are no surcharges and seat reservations are not necessary. The **Italy Flexi Card** offers a similar service but for periods of 4, 8 or 12 days over a one-month duration.

- If you intend to cover great distances by rail you may be interested in the **Biglietto Chilometrico** ticket. The 'kilometric' ticket allows free travel for up to 3,000km and is valid for two months. It can be used by up to five people, but no more than 20 journeys can be made.

- Regular reduced fares are also offered to senior citizens and children under 12, while children under four who do not occupy a seat travel free.

- Discounts are also offered to families and groups of six people and over. Offers are not generally valid for the following periods:
  - from the Friday preceding Palm Sunday to the Sunday after Easter
  - from 25 June to 10 September
  - from 15 December to 10 January.

If you purchase a ticket but do not use it, it is possible to obtain a refund providing you return it to the station from which you bought it on the day for which your ticket is valid. For trains that are delayed for more than 29 minutes, refunds of any supplements or surcharges that have been paid are also offered. The refund will be given in the form of a coupon that can be used on subsequent rail travel. The general information number for the Ferrovie dello Stato is: 8488 88088. Tickets by phone: 199 166 177.

The Ferrovie dello Stato official timetable can be found on the Internet at www.trenitalia.com

Travelling by coach and bus

Local bus networks operate in rural districts, connecting

villages and towns. Tickets are available either from the bus station or on the bus itself. Buses also operate in inner city areas, where bus tickets are sold at major bus stations, *tabacchi* (tobacconists) and sometimes at newspaper kiosks: look for signs saying *'biglietti'*. Tickets are the same price wherever you travel within a city, but if you plan to use city buses regularly you may wish to buy a monthly season ticket *(abbonamento)*. Many cities also have trams which operate on the same ticket system as the buses. Rome, Milan and Naples have a *Metropolitana* (underground train) too. Tickets for the *Metropolitana* are sold at train stations and, like buses, have a flat-rate fare.

Express coach services connect the major cities as well as some of the smaller towns in Italy. Fares are relatively inexpensive and services are operated fairly frequently. Information on timetables is held at local tourist offices and sometimes at local police stations, as well as being posted up at the bus depot itself.

Some coach services also run guided tours both of the local vicinity and as long-distance journeys. The most popular coach trails take in Venice, Padua, Florence, Siena, Perugia, Assisi, Spoleto, Rome, Naples, Pompei, Sorrento, Positano and Amalfi. Typical one-day itineraries are:

- Rome-Naples-Pompeii-Sorrento
- Venice-Padua-Florence, and
- Florence-Siena-Perugia-Assisi-Spoleto-Rome.

For further information you should contact the tourist information centre or a travel agent in the city in which you are staying.

Travelling by ferry

Italy has a good ferry network which operates around its 7,500km of coastline, to and from the two large islands Sardinia and Sicily, and across the northern lakes. The frequency of ferry services to more remote destinations depends on the season.

Sardinia and Sicily
The main crossings for Sardinia are:

- Genoa to Porto Torres/Olbia/Cagliari/Arbatax
- Civitavecchia to Olbia/Cagliari/Arbatax/Golfo Aranci
- Naples to Cagliari
- Livorno to Porto Torres/Golfo Aranci/Olbia.

For Sicily the main crossings are:

- Genoa to Palermo
- Naples to Palermo/Catania/Syracuse
- Livorno to Palermo
- Villa San Giovanni to Messina
- Reggio Calabria to Messina.

There is also a hydrofoil service from Naples to Palermo three times a week, which takes 5 hours 20 minutes. It is also possible to travel from Cagliari in Sardinia to Palermo or Trapani in Sicily.

For information about ferry lines: Tirrenia, Navarma, Adriatica, Torremar, Siemar and Saremar and hydrofoils between The Aeolian islands contract:

SMS Travel and Tourism
40–42 Kenway Road

London SW5 0RA
Tel: 020 7373 6548

From Sicily a ferry service operates from the northern coast to the Aeolian islands. The crossings are operated by the following companies:

Aliscafi SNAV
Via Cortina del Porto
Messina
Tel: 090 364044

SNAV
Agenzia Barbaro
Via Belmonte 51/55
Palermo
Tel: 091 333333

The Bay of Naples
The Bay of Naples is criss-crossed by ferries operating between destinations either side of the bay, and between the mainland and small offshore islands. The principal crossings are:

- Naples to Capri/Ischia/Procida/Sorrento
- Sorrento to Capri.

The companies making these crossings both by ferry and hydrofoil are:

Linea Lauro
Piazza Municipio 88
Napoli
Tel: 081 551 3352
www.lineelauro.it

Caremar Campania Regionale Marittima
Molo Angioino
Naples
Tel: 081 2514721 or 199 123 199 (call centre)

Alilauro
1 Via Caracciolo Francesco
Naples
Tel: 081 382017

Aliscafi SNAV
84 Via Bruno Giordano
Naples
Tel: 081 7612348

Elba
The island of Elba is serviced by car ferry from Piombino
and Livorno, and by hydrofoil from Piombino. The companies operating these services are:

Navarma-Moby Lines.
12 Viale Elba
Portoferraio
Tel: 0565 914133
www.mobylines.it

Toremar
Via Calafati 6
Livorno
Tel: 0586 224511

Toremar
13 Piazzale Premuda

Piombino
Tel: 0565 224859.

Giglio
The island of Giglio, which lies off the Etruscan coast, is connected by car-ferry to Porto Santo Stefano by:

Maregiglio
Via Umberto I, 22
Isola del Giglio, 558013
Tel: 0564 809309
www.maregiglio.it

Adriatic coast
On the Adriatic coast the Adriatica Line runs ferries from Manfredonia, Vieste, Peschici, Rodi Garganico, and Termoli to the Tremiti islands. There is also a hydrofoil to the Tremiti islands from Ortona, Vasto and Termoli.

Northern Lakes
The northern lakes are traversed by umpteen services, including hydrofoils, car-ferries and even steamers.

Lake Maggiore has regular ferries connecting Brissago, Cannobio, Luino, Verbania, Baveno, Stresa, Belgirate, Arona, Locarno, Laveno and others. There is also a hydrofoil service between Arona, Stresa and Locarno, and a car-ferry between Verbania, Intra and Laveno.

Lake Como has steamers, hydrofoils and car-ferries that connect Como, Cernobbio, Carate, Argegno, Tremesso, Cadenabbia, Bellagio, Menaggio, Varenna, Bellano, Colico and others.

Lake Garda has frequent ferries and hydrofoils operating between Riva, Torbole, Limone, Malcesine, Brenzone, Gargnano, Maderno, Gardone, Salo, Garda, Bordolino, Sirmione, Desenzano and Peschiera. There is also a car-ferry between Maderno and Torri del Benaco. Information and bookings:

Navigazione Laghi Maggiore Garda Como
Via L. Aristo 21
20145 Milano
Tel: 02 4676101 or 800 551801
www.navigazionelaghi.it

Travelling by air

The Italian National Carrier, Alitalia, flies to over 100 destinations and its sister company, ATI, operates domestic services between 26 cities in Italy, with the majority of flights centering on Rome (Fiumicino/ Leonardo da Vinci) and Milan (Linate/Malpensa). There are regular flights from Ancona, Bari, Bergamo, Brindisi, Bologna, Catania, Genoa, Firenze, La Mezia Terme, Lampedusa, Naples, Rimini, Parma, Perugia, Pisa, Reggio Calabria, Torino, Trieste, and Venice. Bookings are taken by authorised travel agents in almost any town or city. Before booking your flight check whether you are eligible for one of the following reductions:

- Families travelling together: 50 per cent.
- *'Nastro Verde'* flights at off-peak times: 30 per cent.
- Children up to 2 years old: 90 per cent.
- Children from 2 to 12 years old: 50 per cent.
- Young people aged 12-26: 25 per cent.
- Weekend return flights, travelling on a Saturday or a

Sunday and with no more than four weeks interim: 30 per cent.

- Flights on Sundays, returning the same day: 50 per cent.
- Return flights from North to South Italy: 30 per cent.

The head offices for Alitalia and ATI are:

Alitalia
111 Viale A. Marchetti
00148 Roma
Tel: 06 65621
Information, Tel: 8488 65643
Domestic Reservations, Tel: 06 65641
International Reservations, Tel: 06 65642
www.alitalia.it

Travelling by taxi

Taxis are available in every Italian town. They are usually assembled in ranks in main piazzas, at railway stations and airports, but can also be called by phone. It is not, however, normal to hail a taxi as it passes by. Taxis charge different fares in different places. Official taxis operated by the local comuné show the fare on meter at a rate per kilometer after a fixed starting charge. Extra charges are made for services after 10 at night, and services on Sundays or public holidays. Surcharges are also made for trips outside of a town, such as to an airport, and for luggage.

DRIVING IN ITALY

'When in Rome do as the Romans do' is a saying that may conjure up nightmares when taken in the context of driving in Italy. Driving around in Italy requires a certain amount of bravery, a sharp wit and a good deal of patience. Speed, and small margins for error, seem to be the essence of Italian driving. Overtaking is perhaps the worst aspect, as it is done in dangerous situations with the overtaking driver one minute up your tail, and then a few centimetres to the left of your car, before he swerves in front of you nearly taking off your front bumper. Another nightmare of the road is the signposting. Signs are terrible and it can be enormously difficult to find the correct road, even with a good map. Quite often the junction is signposted only at the actual turning and not in advance, and there may be a display of 20 signs to scan through, including those for hotels, restaurants, businesses and public services. It is far from uncommon to find two signs for the same destination pointing in opposite directions; sometimes all roads do lead to Rome!

To add to this, most roads around big towns and cities are very busy, while the centres themselves are positively traffic-choked. Nearly all Italians have at least one car per family and many have two, or even three. Road congestion is not the only problem. Car parking is a headache almost everywhere, and when the winter brings fog and mist to the cities of Northern Italy there is the problem of car exhaust-enhanced smog too. When pollution levels reach an unbearable limit cars are restricted by allowing number plates ending in an even number on the roads one day and those ending in an odd number on the next. Sometimes vehicles are banned from using the roads altogether.

Getting around by car does, however, have its advantages, and if you intend to buy a rural property in Italy you may find that it is essential.

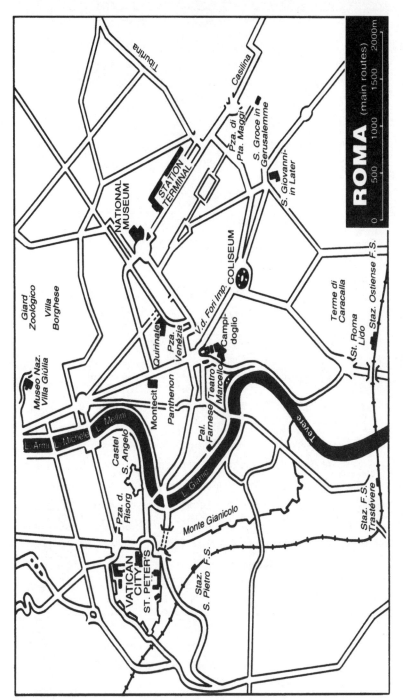

Fig. 2. Rome city plan.

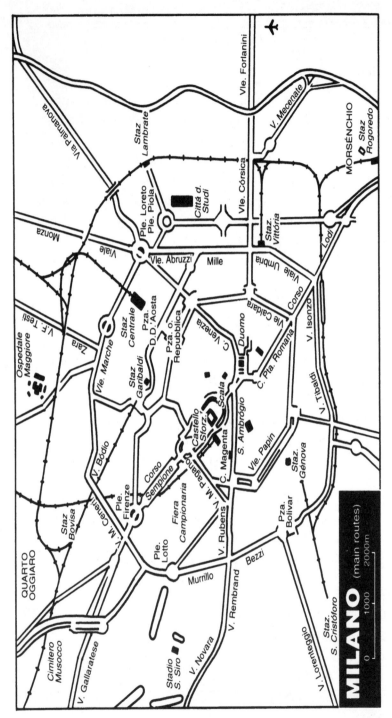

Fig. 3. Milan city plan.

Hiring a car

Major international as well as Italian car-hire companies are represented at all airports and major railway stations throughout Italy, but in order to hire a car you must have had a full driving licence for at least one year. Most companies stipulate that the driver must be over 19 years old, and a 1993 law states that drivers who have had their licences for less than three years are not allowed to drive vehicles with a speed capacity of over 150km per hour.

Hire rates vary from company to company and from car to car, but it is rarely cheap and you will be lucky if you can find a car for much under £200 per week. When you ask for a quote check that it includes breakdown service, maintenance, oil and basic insurance. Find out the cost of additional insurance, and remember that 20 per cent IVA (VAT) will be added to your final bill. It is normal for a company to ask for a deposit which is equal to the estimated cost of the car-hire. Car-hire firms in tourist centres and cities also usually rent out mopeds, motorbikes and sometimes bicycles too.

Transhire, one of the longest established hire brokers in the UK, represents the Italian car hire firm Maggiore, offering competitive rates: a 3-door Fiat Punto is approximately £169 per week in winter and £172 per week in summer.

Transhire
Unit 16
88 Clapham Park Road
London SW4 7BX
Tel: 0870 789 8000
www.transhire.com

Head offices of major car hire firms in Italy are:

Avis
1231 Via Tiburtina
Rome
Tel: 06 41998
www.avis.com

Hertz
Viale Shakespeare, 43
Rome
Tel: 06 5922742
www.hertz.com

Europcar
Via Fiume Giallo
Rome
Tel: 06 520811
www.europcar.com

Maggiore Autonoleggio
225 Via di Tor Cervara
Rome
Tel: 06 2291530
www.maggiore.it

Buying a car in Italy

In order to buy a car in Italy you must be registered as a local
resident and be in possession of a **codice fiscale** (fiscal code
number).

A point to check before buying a car is whether its road tax has been paid. If a car has been off the road for some time, the chances are that the road tax payments have not been maintained. If this is the case you will find that you are liable for back payments when you go to renew the road tax.

The procedure for buying a car is quite straightforward. You will need to present your resident's certificate and fiscal code number. If you are buying a car privately take these documents and go to a local office of the Automobile Club Italiano (ACI) with the seller. The necessary documents will be drawn up for the transfer of ownership, known as 'Trapasso'.

If you are a non-resident you can only purchase a brand new vehicle which is intended for export within a year of purchase. Failure to export in time can result in the vehicle being seized and the driver given a hefty fine.

Running a car in Italy

The two major costs involved in running a car in Italy, other than fuel, repair and maintenance, are insurance and road tax. Car MOTs (revisione) only apply to cars more than 10 years old. Cars over 5 years old are tested for fume emissions and issued with 'bollino blu'.

Insurance
Every vehicle must have basic third party insurance, proof of which is displayed in the car windscreen. Car insurance is obtainable from the Automobile Club Italiano and from insurance agents.

There are two types of insurance, *franchigia* and *bonus/malus*. The former type of policy is now less common and is only offered by the largest insurance companies and to heavy goods vehicles. A *franchigia* policy means that the driver pays for damage costs up to a certain amount, over and above which the insurance company takes responsibility. Far more common is the *bonus/malus* policy which operates on a no claims bonus system. A new driver starts with 18 points, others enter at number 14 and for each year that you do not claim you lose a point. If you have an accident you gain two points.

The obligatory basic insurance only offers third party and members of family who are travelling in the car. The driver is covered by taking out a supplement for *conducente anonimo* (unnamed driver) which will also pay for hospital treatment in case of an accident. Insurance against theft and fire put up the cost of the policy considerably. However, if you are in a city, particularly in the south of Italy, it is probably worth paying for as car theft is very commonplace. In the large Italian cities there is one car stolen every 90 seconds. The city of Cagliari in Sardinia is said to be the most active centre, as vehicles are shipped out from there to Turkey and the Gulf. You may also be interested to know that Fiat 500s and Fiat Unos are especially popular with car thieves.

Road tax
Road tax now includes the Driving Licence Fee and is payable every three, six or 12 months at your local PTT (post office). The *bollo* (chit) with which you make the payment is available from Automobile Club Italiano (ACI) offices (www.aci.it). However, if your car has been in circulation in

Italy for any length of time you should have received a supply of *bolli* (chits) in the form of a large cheque book. Each
bollo is valid for three months. The *bollo* should be renewed
within the first two weeks following the month of expiring,
ie if it is valid for October, then the next tax must be paid by
14 November. The *bollo* must be filled in using the information on the charts you will find up on the wall in any post
office, the idea being to calculate the amount of tax you must
pay. This depends on the type of fuel that is used, the horse-
power category of the engine and the length of time for
which you wish to tax the car. See the model *bollo* on
page 64.

Once your *bollo* is completed take it to any counter that is not
reserved for postal transactions and pay the final figure. You
will be given a receipt which acts as your tax disc and must
be displayed alongside your insurance in your windscreen.

If you are still in the process of converting your British-registered car to Italian plates and your British road tax has
expired, you should apply to an Automobile Club Italiano
(ACI) office for a temporary road tax cover. This costs considerably less than the full road tax. However, in theory it can
only be issued for three months, although in practice it seems
it can be renewed almost indefinitely.

Fuel

Italian petrol (*benzina*) is considerably less expensive than in
the UK. Unleaded (*'verde' or 'senza piombo'*) comes in two
octane ratings 95 and 98. Diesel (*gasolio*) is cheaper than
petrol and is widely available. LPG–Liquid Petroleum Gas
(*GPL*) is increasingly favoured, due to its lower price and

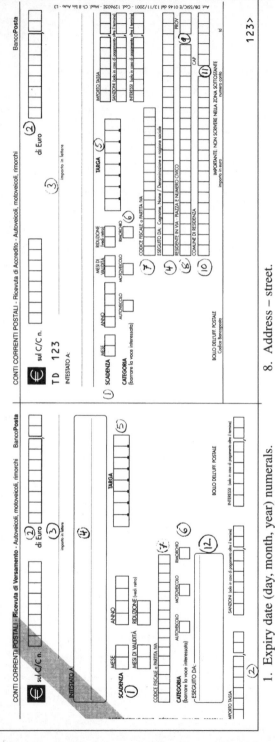

1. Expiry date (day, month, year) numerals.
2. Total amount of tax paid in numerals.
3. Total amount of tax paid in letters.
4. Full name of car owner.
5. Number plate.
6. Category – car, motorbike or trailer.
7. Personal Italian tax code number.
8. Address – street.
9. Province initials.
10. Place.
11. Post code.
12. Valid from.

Fig. 4. Form for paying car tax.

environmental friendliness, and available at petrol stations showing the GPL sign. However if you are resident in Italy it may only be cheaper to run a diesel car if you travel extensively as a higher road tax is levied.

Opening hours of petrol stations do vary from place to place, but in general most open from 7.30 am to 12.30 pm and then take two or three hours for lunch, re-opening around 3 pm until 7 pm. Only 25 per cent of petrol stations are open on Sundays and public holidays. Many are closed on Mondays too or for one other week day. However, petrol stations on motorways, which can be found every 25km, stay open 24 hours a day. Some non-motorway petrol stations also have automatic pumps which operate 24 hours a day and accept credit and debit cards.

THE RULES OF THE ROAD

Road regulations

The first thing to remember about driving in Italy is to keep to the right-hand side of the road and give way to traffic from the right on roundabouts and at crossroads. If you have a right-hand drive car you will find the left-hand wing mirror indispensable; it is anyway obligatory to have one. It is also obligatory to carry a warning triangle in your boot and to have your driving licence and car registration documents on you at all times.

Road signs are international and driving rules conform to European standards, although in practice little regard is given to pedestrian crossings, and traffic from the right often takes precedence. The degree to which driving rules are obeyed and enforced varies greatly across the country. Naples can seem to be virtually law-free at times, with neither traffic lights nor one-way streets being respected.

Children under four must be strapped into a car safety seat, and children aged between four and 12 must wear a child's safety restraint. Drunken driving is a grave offence, although breathalising is nothing like as common as in the UK and safe limits do not really exist. Fines are paid on the spot, usually after the driver has pleaded innocence and tried to knock down the cost of the fine. If you are unable to pay a fine you are given 60 days in which to honour your debt. A list of the most common offences and the fines they incur is given below.

Speeding up to 10km/h above the limit:	32 Euros
Speeding up to 40km/h above the limit:	131 Euros
Speeding 40km/h above the limit:	262 Euros
	plus suspension of licence
Driving on wrong side of road on a bend or in a place with poor visibility:	131 Euros
	plus suspension of licence
Not observing road signs:	32 Euros
Not giving way:	65 Euros
Going through a red light:	65 Euros
Overtaking on the inside:	32 Euros
Overtaking on a bend or hill:	65 Euros
Not maintaining a safe distance:	32 Euros
Misuse of lights:	65 Euros
Changing direction without signalling:	32 Euros
Disturbing the peace:	32 Euros
Stopping at a forbidden place:	32 Euros

Carrying more passengers than permitted: 32 Euros
Carrying a passenger on a moped: 32 Euros
Under-age driving: Seizure of vehicle
Not wearing a helmet: 32 Euros
Not wearing a safety belt: 32 Euros
Not carrying licence or circulation documents: 32 Euros
Carrying an out of date licence: 131 Euros
plus withdrawal of licence

Speed limits

Speed limits are marked on road signs and should be observed carefully, although they rarely are by Italians. The limits are:

- in built-up areas 50km per hour
- on country roads 90km per hour
- on the motorway: for cars up to 1100cc and motorcycles up to 350cc 110km per hour; for cars over 1100cc and motorcycles over 350cc 130km per hour
- towing a caravan or trailer: outside built-up areas 80km per hour; on the motorways 100km per hour.

Different limits are often set for weekends and public holidays. For variations in speed limits watch out for the illuminated signs on motorways, which also indicate road and traffic conditions, etc.

Drivers help one another not to be caught speeding by flashing their lights when the police are around on most roads, but on motorways of course this is not possible and state of the art radar traps are used. The automatic detector photographs the speeding vehicle and dispatches a fine through the post.

However, with the Italians' uncanny knack of wriggling out of most situations, the driver often denies responsibility, since the detector records the number plate and not the identity of the driver. The fine is payable by the person under whose name the vehicle is registered, not who was driving. A great number of high-power cars are therefore registered under the names of the geriatric members of a family. Hence Italy has a record high number of law-breaking elderly people.

Parking

Finding a place to park is a problem in all Italian towns and cities. The medieval streets that characterise so many of Italy's towns were not designed to accommodate the hordes of cars that now flood them. Parking meters are often posted along narrow streets that radiate out from the town centre, but these spaces are invariably full. Small fee-paying car-parks are also usually dotted around a centre, but like parking meters there is generally a 90-minute limit and the spaces are quickly filled. You will also find areas that are marked *zona disco* or *zona blu*. A **disco** is a parking disc with a clock face on which you can indicate the time you arrived. If you do not have one, apply to the Automobile Club Italiano (ACI), the tourist office or a petrol station. Parking in a *zona disco* obliges you to use the disc and to return within the time limit that is indicated, which varies from 20 minutes to an hour. The actual centre of many towns is closed to all traffic during working hours, except for residents and public transport. This exacerbates the parking problem, but of course makes for blissfully traffic-free town centres. In the centre of Rome parking is strictly prohibited on weekdays and is indicated by signs reading *zona tutelato*. In Florence all vehicles are banned from the centre from 7.30 am to 6.30 pm on week-days except for access. Venice has overcome its parking problems by building multi-storey carparks which are linked by ferry and bus services to destinations in Venice, but charges are exorbitant. Most large cities also have private garages which rent out space by the day and guarantee the safety of your car. Car parks with a custodian offer the same security, with fees usually charged by the hour. If you park your car at the side of a road make sure it is on the right side and facing the oncoming traffic.

Do not park where you see the signs *passo carrabile, divieto di sosta*, or *sosta vietato* as this means you will be blocking an entrance or a right of way. Neither should you park where you see the sign *zona rimozione* which means your car will be towed away. Should your car be towed away, go to the *Vigili Urbani* (police). You will be charged from 32-65 Euros to reclaim it, plus a fee for its storage.

If you receive a parking ticket take it to the police station, or pay a policeman on duty. The fine should be paid within 60 days. An example of a parking ticket is given in Figure 5 and shows a list of typical offences, each of which incurs a charge of up to 65 Euros. You should also note the new parking reg-ulation which states that where there is no pavement drivers must park 1m from the side of the road in order to allow pedestrians a right of way.

Car theft

If you have your car stolen while you are in Italy you should go to the nearest police station. The thieves may try to inter-vene before you get to the police and offer to return your car for a sum of money. However, accepting bribes does not

PREAVVISO DI ACCERTAMENTO D'INFRAZIONE AL c.d.s.

1   2   3

In data .... *alle ore* .... *in via* ....

.... *n.* .... *il sottoscritto Vigile Urbano ha accertato che il*
4   5
veicolo .... *targato* ....
6
era in sosta violando il disposto contrassegnato con X

ART. 7

7 ❑ sosta - fermata in luogo vietato indicato da apposito segnale

8 ❑ sosta in ore - divieto per pulizia strade

9 ❑ sosta senza esposizione biglietto orario di arrivo

10 ❑ avendo pagato sostava oltre il tempo consentito

11 ❑ sosta fuori degli appositi spazi

12 ❑ in zona disco - oltre l'orario di scadenza

ART. 157

13 ❑ in zona disco - disco non esposto

14 ❑ in zona disco - impiego errato del disco

15 ❑ sosta in direzione contraria al senso di marcia

16 ❑ sosta non sul margine della carreggiata

17 ❑ sosta non parallelamente all'asse stradale

18 ❑ sosta senza lasciare spazio per il transito dei pedoni

19 ❑ sosta senza lasciare spazio per il transito dei veicoli

ART. 158

20 ❑ sosta nella zona a traffico limitato

21 ❑ sosta che impedisce l'accesso o l'uscita ad altro veicolo regolarmente parheggiato

22 ❑ sosta negli attraversamenti pedonali

23 ❑ sosta in seconda fila

24 ❑ sosta in prossimità - corrispondenza aree inters., curva, dossi, ecc.

25 ❑ sosta su spazi riservati

a ....

26 ❑ sosta davanti cassonetto o contenitore analogo raccolta rifiuti

27 ❑ sosta allo sbocco di passo carrabile

28 ❑ sosta con le ruota sul marciapiede

❑ ....

❑ ....

❑ ....

29   **IL VIGILE URBANO** ....

AVVERTENZA: Poiché non è stato possibile contestare immediatamente la presente violazione, il relativo verbale sarà notificato all'intestatario de documento di circolazione o proprietario del veicolo, a meno che il trasgressore al fine di evitare le spese di notificazione non voglia versare

30

ENTRO 15 GIORNI dalla data sopraindicata la somma di € ...., dovuta per oblazione in via breve: presso qualsiasi Ufficio Postale, servendosi dell'allegato modulo di c/c **n. 13064621**, o al Comando VV.UU. di questo Comune.

1. Date	17. Parked without being parallel to the road
2. Time	18. Parked without leaving space for pedestrians
3. Street	
4. Vehicle	19. Parked without leaving room for for passing traffic
5. Number plate	
6. Contravention of parking regulation marked X	20. Parked in a limited traffic zone
	21. Parked restricting access of other parked vehicles
7. Parked in a forbidden place	
8. Parked during forbidden times	22. Parked on a pedestrian crossing
9. Parked without displaying arrival time	23. Parked in outside lane
10. Parked after paid time expired	24. Parked near intersection, bends etc.
11. Parked outside allotted space	25. Parked in reserved spaces for . . .
12. Parked in disc zone after expiry time	26. Parked against refuse bins
13. Parked in disc zone without displaying disc	27. Parked blocking a right of way
14. Parked in disc zone with disc incorrectly adjusted	28. Parked with wheels on pavement
15. Parked against oncoming traffic	29. Signature of town parking warden
16. Parked too far from the side of the road	30. Amount due before 15 days from date above – in any post office

Fig. 5. Parking ticket and offences.

secure the safe return of your vehicle. At the police station you will have to complete a *denuncia* which is a legal report that will eventually be read before a court of justice if necessary. You will not be able to make an insurance claim in Italy until the court has decreed the vehicle as stolen; until that point it is merely missing. Should your car be found again, the police will keep it impounded until you are ready to collect it. Before taking your vehicle back you will have to go to the police and complete another *denuncia*, stating that the vehicle has been recovered. If the vehicle has any damage make sure that it is written on this report as this will enable you to make an insurance claim.

Motorways

Italy has a good network of motorways, covering over 6,000km. Tolls are charged on all motorways except the one between Salerno and Reggio Calabria, which is also one of the most spectacular in Italy, those in Sicily between Palermo and Mazara del Vallo, and some short sections outside some of the larger cities.

Motorways are indicated by green signposts with white lettering, the particular motorway being designated by 'A' for *autostrada*, followed by the motorway number. Care should be taken on the motorways themselves, as often the exit signs appear only seconds before, or even at, the exit itself which can make for some rapid manoeuvering.

Before joining a motorway you must take a ticket from an automatic dispenser. Keep the ticket carefully as it has to be presented when you come off the motorway. The toll is calculated according to the type of vehicle you are travelling in and the distance you have covered. If you lose your ticket you will be charged for the maximum possible distance travelled on that motorway. If you intend to use the motorway regularly you may wish to purchase a **Viacard** or a **Telepass**. These are available from the motorway toll booths and service areas, Automobile Club Italiano (ACI), some banks and at *tabacchi* (tobacconists) in major towns. The cards are sold in denominations of 25, 50 and 70 Euros and the card is valid until the credit is used up. In order to pay with a *Viacard* or *Telepass* get in the correct lane at the toll station and feed the card into the automatic machine. At toll stations without automatic barriers simply hand the card to the attendant or obtain an electronic payment device to fit onto your windscreen from any Punto Blu service station by showing your Viacard and quoting your vehicle registration number for a small charge of 1.03 Euros a month.

If you break down on the motorway, make sure your hazard lights are on and your warning triangle is positioned at least 150m from your vehicle before heading for one of the SOS call boxes which are located at intervals of 2km. There are two types of call boxes; one is a regular phone into which you can speak, the other is a press button device which gives you the choice of alerting either the mechanical breakdown service or the Red Cross for ambulance service. The Automobile Club Italiano also operate a breakdown service which can be called by dialling 116.

Information on road conditions is transmitted by the radio stations RAI 1, 2 and 3 at half-hourly intervals in French, German and English. The reports are known as ***Onda Verde*** and ***Onda Verde Europa*** and are transmitted on frequencies

FM and AM 103.5. Information is also broadcast through the televideo channel on TV, page 485 for normal road conditions, and page 495 for motorway conditions. By telephone dial 06 43632121 or 06 43634363 for the latest road reports. You will also find information in service areas where there is a televideo screen and the *Punti Blu* which are indicated by a large blue dot. When driving conditions are abnormal overhead signs are illuminated on the motorway itself and at the entry point to the system.

Most motorway service stations have snack-bars. The system is to go to the cash till before consuming anything, collect a receipt for the things you want to buy, then present the receipt to the bar-person who will make up your order. Service stations have restaurants, toilets, telephones and sometimes shops selling local produce.

Italian motorways
A comprehensive list of Italy's motorways, many of which are named after ancient Roman routes, is given below:

A1   Milan-Rome-Naples (Autostrada del Sole)
A3   Naples-Salerno-Reggio Calabria (Autostrada del Sole)
A4   Turin-Trieste (Serenissima)
A5   Turin-Aosta
A6   Turin-Savona
A7   Milan-Genoa
A8   Milan-Varese (Autostrada dei Laghi)
A9   Milan-Como-Chiasso (Autostrada dei Laghi)
A10   Genoa-Ventimiglia (Autostrada dei Fiori)
A11   Florence-Pisa (Firenze Mare)
A12   Genoa-Rome (Autostrada Azzurra)
A13   Bologna-Padua

A14 Bologna-Bari-Taranto (Autostrada Adriatica)
A15 Parma-La Spezia (Autostrada della Cisa)
A16 Naples-Bari (Autostrada dei due Mari)
A18 Messina-Catania
A19 Palermo-Catania
A20 Messina-Buonfornello
A21 Turin-Piacenza-Brescia (Autostrada dei Vini)
A22 Brennero-Modena (Autostrada del Brennero)
A23 Udine-Tarvisio (Autostrada Alpe-Adria)
A24 Rome-l'Aquila-Teramo
A25 Rome Pescara
A26 Genoa-Gravellona (Autostrada dei Trafori)
A27 Venice-Vittorio Veneto (Autostrada d'Alemagna)
A28 Portogruaro-Pordenone
A29 Palermo-Mazara del Vallo
A30 Caserta-Nola-Salerno
A31 Vicenza-Rovigo (Autostrada della Valdastico)
A32 Turin-Bardonecchia
T1   Traforo del Monte Bianco
T2   Traforo del Gran San Bernardo
T4   Traforo del Frejus

Italian road signs

Some of the most common road signs are:

entrata	entrance
incrocio	crossroads
lavori in corso	road works ahead
luci	lights
passaggio a livello	level crossing
pericolo	danger
rallentare	slow down
senso vietato	no entry

senso unico	one way
sosta autorizzata	parking permitted at indicated times
sosta vietato	no parking
strada privata	private road
uscita	exit
vietato ingresso	no entry
vietato transito autocarri	closed to heavy vehicles.

CASE HISTORY: CATCHING THE FERRY

A family booked tickets for the ferry to Elba, but made a mistake with their dates, so that the rented accommodation dates did not correspond to those of the ferry dates. Unsure of what to do they contemplated trying to explain what had happened to the ferry company, but remembering that they were in Italy they decided to play it another way. They roughed up their ticket a bit so that the date was indistinct and turned up very early on the day they wished to travel back to mainland Italy, rather than on the day they had booked. There was the usual confusion at the ferry terminal and not only did they get to travel when they wanted, but even boarded an earlier ferry than they should have.

Advice: honesty is not *always* the best policy!

④

Practical Matters

DAY-TO-DAY LIVING
Banks and money

Although the banking system in Italy is somewhat antiquated, the pressure of the European Union free market has obliged banks to develop computer link-ups and install automatic cash machines to deal with everyday transactions. The banking system is still limited, however, by virtue of the fact that the majority of banks are local and not national. There are therefore difficulties in obtaining services at any other bank than your own, the branches of which are probably limited to the province or region. A credit card, Eurocheques, or travellers' cheques are therefore essential when travelling.

To open a bank account you will have to meet the bank manager, or his secretary, and if you can arrange for someone to introduce you or recommend you, all the better. You have to win the confidence of the bank manager, which means letting him get to know you, because the bank can find itself responsible for your personal debts. As well as being asked questions about yourself, you will probably have to show your resident's certificate, your fiscal code card and your passport. Once you have a current bank account you may wish to request an automatic cash card, such as Bancomat, and a cheque book. Cheques have a limited value as they are often not accepted by people who do not know you, especially outside your own region. More versatile is a credit/charge card, such as Carta Si, which is very flexible but comes with an annual charge.

If you have an Italian cheque book fill it in as shown in Figure 6. You will find that it is very common to leave who the cheque is payable to and also the date blank. You should also write *non-trasferibile* across the back of the cheque.

A bank account can be used to pay standing charges, such as telephone, electricity and gas bills, and to receive bank transfers from an overseas account. The disadvantages of opening a bank account are the numerous charges and taxes that are automatically deducted every year. A regular annual tax of around 20 per cent is directly debited, while an annual interest of around 3.5 per cent is credited. Commission is usually charged at about 0.5 per cent. It is also normal to pay for each cheque you write, as well as the cheque book itself and credit card transactions. Added to this there are *straordinario* (extraordinary) charges, such as when, in the summer of 1992, recession hit Italy and the Government levied a tax of 0.6 per cent on all current accounts. You may decide in the end to do without an Italian bank account altogether! All charges and other transactions are written on a monthly statement. The facsimile in Figure 7 may help you to decipher it.

If you are not a resident of Italy it is possible to open a foreigner's account. However, charges and taxes are higher than those for residents and should most definitely be checked beforehand. You should also check the facilities that are available. It is not, for example, possible to pay standing charges with a foreigner's account.

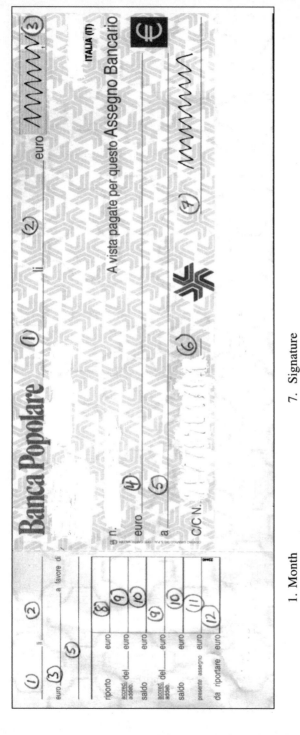

1. Month
2. Date
3. Amount in numerals
4. Amount in words
5. Payable to
6. Account number

7. Signature
8. Amount carried forward
9. Credit or debits
10. Balance
11. This cheque
12. Balance to carry forward

Fig. 6. Filling in a cheque.

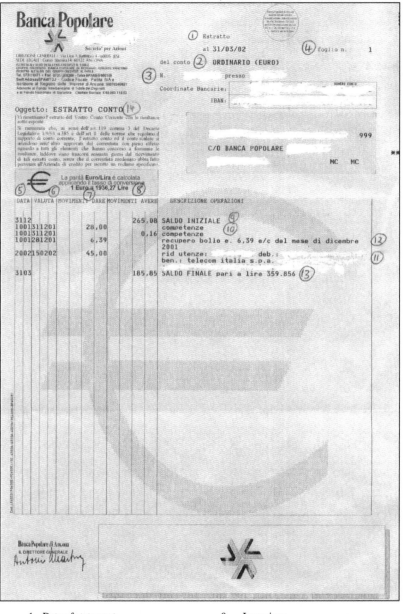

1. Date of statement
2. Type of account
3. Number and place of account
4. Page number
5. Date
6. Validity date
7. Outgoings
8. Incomings
9. Starting balance
10. Fees
11. Standing order telecom for Italia
12. Postage and tax costs
13. Final balance
14. Account extract

Fig. 7. Bank statement.

Most banks are open Monday to Friday 8.30 am - 1.30 pm
and 3-4 pm, but hours do vary slightly from bank to bank,
and some do not reopen in the afternoon at all. Every bank
has an individual security door mechanism which involves
pressing buttons, waiting before being able to enter, and
passing through a metal detector (there are usually boxes in
which to deposit metal objects such as car keys, etc). Inside
the bank, money is handled at a reinforced-glass *cassa*,
cash desk, while transactions are dealt with over the counter.
This means that once you have completed a transaction
you must then queue at the cash desk if you are receiving
money.

Post offices

The PTT or *Ufficio Postale*, as the post office is called in
Italy, is the nerve centre of Italian bureaucracy. It is here that
you queue for your pension, your car tax, telephone and electricity bills and any of the miscellany of taxes that are
payable by postal order. The post office of course also operates a variety of postal services which are usually available at
a separate desk. If you simply want to buy a postage stamp
(francobollo) you will probably find it quicker to go to a
tabacchi (tobacconist), although if the letter is to be sent at a
special rate the tobacconist may not be able to deal with it.
Tobacconists do not deal with parcels either. To send a parcel
you must fill in a form at the post office giving details of both
the sender *(mittente)* and the receiver *(destinatario)*. If the
parcel is to be sent overland, you may have to go to the parcel section of the post office. Most post offices are fussy
about the way in which you package a parcel: the preferred
method is to use string and a metal seal which can be

purchased from a *cartolibreria* (book shop) or *tabacchi* (tobacconists).

Other services offered by the post office include sending telegrams and receiving mail by *poste restante.* To receive correspondence by *poste restante* the sender should write *fermo posta* before the address of the post office. The post office also deals with money orders of various types. Authorised international reimbursements (ARI) and guaranteed payment papers (CPG) can be arranged telegraphically or by normal post, as well as international money orders. In order to cash money orders you will need to show your passport or identity card.

Information regarding postal services is obtainable by dialling 160.

Public telephones

Telephone booths are found in all town centres and in or near major post offices. Public telephones are also installed in cafes, and in remote country areas you will find authorised persons who have a phone for public use — look for the telephone symbol fixed to their house.

In order to operate a pay-phone you need either coins or a phone card. Phone cards, which are sold for 2.50 or 5 Euros are available from *tabacchi* (tobacconists) or from SIP *(Societa Italiana Telefoni Pubblici)* offices. Phones in cafes and private homes usually operate on meters. The cost of the call is calculated by the number of *scatti* (points) that are registered on the meter. Cafes also sometimes add a supplementary charge for the use of the phone. The dialling tone sounds 'tu-tuuu'. When you hear 'tuuu' repeated at intervals it means the number is ringing. The continuous sound 'tu-tu-tu' means the number is engaged.

The charges made for using the telephone depend on the time of day and the distance. The categorisation of distance is as follows:

- inter-urban
- up to 15km
- from15km to 30km
- from 30km to 60km
- from 60km to 120km
- over 120km.

The tariffs for the times of the day are organised as below:

- Peak hour, Monday–Friday 8.30 am – 1 pm: 150 per cent.

- Ordinary, Monday–Friday 8–8.30 am and 1–6.30 pm; Saturday 8 am – 1 pm: 100 per cent.

- Reduced, Monday–Friday 6.30–10 pm; Saturday 1–10 pm: Sunday and public holidays 8 am – 10 pm; 70 per cent.

- Economy, daily 10 pm – 8 am: 50 per cent.

You will find local telephone directories, known as **elenchi telefonici,** anywhere that has a public phone. Complete sets of telephone directories covering all of Italy's provinces are usually held by the tourist office and SIP offices. Failing that, directory enquiries can be obtained by dialling 12.

Making international calls

If you want to book an international call dial 170. The personnel speak both French and English and operate a 24-hour service.

If you want to make a direct international call, dial 00 and then the prefix of the country to which you are making the phone call. This should be followed by the area code, and then the actual telephone number. A list of international prefixes is given below:

Austria	43
Belgium	32
Denmark	45
Egypt	20
Finland	358
France	33
Germany	37
Greece	30
Ireland	353
Luxembourg	352
Malta	356
Morocco	212
Netherlands	31
Norway	47
Portugal	351
Spain	34
Sweden	46
Switzerland	41
Tunisia	216
Turkey	90
UK	44

Shopping

The opening hours of shops in Italy may take some time to adjust to. Generally they:

- open at 8.30 or 9 in the morning
- close at 12.30 or 1 for lunch
- re-open at 4.30 or 5 in the afternoon
- close at 7.30 or 8 in the evening.

These are the standard opening hours from Monday to Saturday inclusive, all shops being closed on Sunday, except for fresh pasta shops which open on Sunday morning. While this is quite straightforward, figuring out the early closing days is more difficult. Generally speaking all shops that sell food close on a Wednesday or Thursday afternoon, although in some regions it is Tuesday. Hardware stores and shops selling appliances or machinery usually close on Saturday afternoons. Butchers often close for two afternoons in a week, usually on a Tuesday and Thursday. This should logically leave Monday as an ideal time to find all the shops open. However, Monday is frequently the closing day for places such as hairdressers, photographers, clothes boutiques and pasta shops. In the summer everybody takes a three-week holiday some time between June and October, the favourite month being August. You will find *chiuso per ferie* written on the shop doors, with the date on which it will reopen. In tourist resorts the opposite applies. Shops stay open at all hours and on all days of the week, even on national holidays, particularly if they occur during a peak tourist season.

Unlike Britain, the town centres in Italy are not dominated by faceless shopping precincts and chain stores. Supermarkets are commonplace, but they are often quite small and do not have a meat department. Most supermarkets are franchises, such as Sidis, Cral and Conad, and stock a mixture of their own and other brands as well as local produce. Small grocery stores, *alimentari*, and butchers, *macellerie*, also sell local fare and generally take pride in the quality of their products. Bakers usually bake on the premises, producing a variety of breads and rolls as well as biscuits and cakes. Patisserie and cream cakes tend to be sold in cafes. All towns also have at least one fresh pasta shop where numerous varieties of pasta are made daily.

You will be given a receipt, *ricevuta fiscale*, with all purchases, which you should keep until reaching home. The *guardia di finanza*, a branch of the police, have the right to demand to see receipts for any goods you have on you or in your vehicle, and in the unlikely event of this happening and your not having the receipt both you and the seller can be lumbered with a fine.

Some of the shops you will come across include:

alimentari	food shop/grocery
antiquario	antique dealer
calzolaio	shoe repairer
casa del formaggio	cheese shop
casa di pasta	fresh pasta shop
enoteca	wine merchant
farmacia	chemist
ferramenta	hardware store
gelateria	icecream shop
gioielleria	jeweller
macelleria	butcher

mercato	market
paneficio/panetteria	bakery
parrucchiere	hairdresser
pasticceria	cake shop
pescheria	fish shop
profumeria	perfume shop
salumeria	salami and cured meats
supermercato	supermarket
tabacchi	tobacconist
tintoria	dry cleaners
ufficio postale	post office

You will find that most towns do not have launderettes but only dry cleaners. Some dry cleaners take in regular washing but it is an expensive habit to get into. Nearly all Italian families have a washing machine in their homes so launderettes are only found in the biggest cities and where there is a high student or tourist population, such as in Florence.

Public conveniences

Public conveniences come under a host of different names, including:

- *gabinetti*
- *toiletta*
- *bagno*
- *WC.*

Ladies is *signore* and Gentlemen is *signori*. You may also find the toilets labelled *donna* for women and *uomo* for men. If you cannot find a public convenience in the town, bars and cafes always have a bathroom for public use and usually do not mind you using it even if you are not a customer.

Household bills

If you are running a home in Italy you will be paying bills six times a year for your electricity, gas and telephone. There are standing charges for each of these services, so even if you are not living in your Italian home all year round you will still have bills to pay. The easiest way to pay bills is to have them directly debited from your Italian bank account. Otherwise you can pay bills at the bank or post office. To avoid the small surcharge that this incurs you may prefer to pay your bills to the appropriate local office. For the telephone go to a SIP office, for electricity find an ENEL office and for mains gas pay at the local Metano office.

Keep a record of all bills that you have paid in case you need to prove their payment at any time. You may also need to contest your bill. Electricity and gas are assessed according to an estimated consumption rather than to a meter reading. Twice a year you receive a bill, called *conguaglio*, which settles the difference between the estimated and actual consumption. This is either a nasty shock or a pleasant surprise. Should you be in credit you will receive the difference by postal order which can be cashed at the post office.

To understand exactly what is written on your bill examples for electricity, telephone and gas are shown in Figures 8, 9 and 10.

The press

Newspapers in Italy are read widely, but are not delivered to

 **Enel Distribuzione**
ZONA DI MACERATA
Via Roma 157 - 62100 MACERATA (1)

Il suo numero cliente è _____ (5)

CODICE FISCALE: . (30)

TASSA PAGATA FATTURE CONVENZIONE NAZIONALE DEL 1/3/1999

(2) *presso* C.O Bca Pop.

ENEL DISTRIBUZIONE S.P.A.
SEDE LEGALE VIA OMBRONE, 2 - 00198 ROMA
REG.IMPRESE DI ROMA, C.F. e P.I. 05779971000 - R.E.A. 922436
CAPITALE SOCIALE Euro 6.119.200.000 l. v.

Bolletta per la fornitura di energia elettrica
Bimestre novembre - dicembre 2001

Le stiamo fornendo energia in

(6) per usi domestici
per abitazione di residenza
con tariffa D2
(7) con potenza contrattualmente
impegnata di 3 kW (chilowatt)
e potenza disponibile
di 3,3 kW (chilowatt)

(4) Abbiamo calcolato questa bolletta tenendo conto dei suoi consumi abituali. Quindi consideriamo che il **07/12/2001** il suo contatore abbia segnato **10562** scatti.

Dall'altra parte del foglio troverà il dettaglio delle letture, del consumo calcolato e dei prezzi applicati.

Il totale da pagare entro il 27/12/2001 (23) è di euro:
10,76 (26)

(lire 20.834)
Come da lei richiesto, sarà addebitato nel giorno esatto della scadenza su conto corrente presso:
Banca Popolare (22)

(15)

LETTURA DEL CONTATORE
Gentile cliente, di norma leggiamo i contatori una volta all'anno. Tra una lettura e l'altra emettiamo bollette di acconto calcolando una media dei consumi dei lei effettuati nel periodo precedente. Per la prossima bolletta, se non è disponibile una lettura, prevediamo che il **26/01/2002** il suo contatore segnerà **10586** scatti. Se prima di questa data, lei vede sul suo contatore una cifra molto diversa, può comunicarcela usando **Eneltel.** Le istruzioni sono qui a fianco. Correggeremo la nostra previsione tenendo conto di detta lettura.

COME USARE ENELTEL
Ecco come può telefonarci la sua lettura: si scriva il numero degli scatti che appare sul contatore. Se dopo una virgola c'è una cifra, non la consideri. (16) Faccia il numero telefonico **16444.** Sentirà una voce che le dirà di comporre sul suo telefono: (17)
→ il suo numero cliente (
→ e, poi, il numero degli scatti del contatore. Avrà conferma immediata del ricevimento della sua lettura, o eventuali altre istruzioni.
La telefonata le costa uno scatto solo, da qualsiasi località d'Italia. (15)

PRONTOENEL
Per quanto riguarda il **contratto,** la **bolletta, le informazioni** e i **reclami** può telefonare al numero verde **800-900106** . Una persona è a sua disposizione dalle 8.00 alle 20.00 da lunedì a venerdì e dalle 8.00 alle 18.00 il sabato. Per le **informazioni,** il servizio con risponditore automatico, è attivo tutti i giorni 24 ore su 24.

GUASTI
Per **segnalare un guasto** telefoni al numero verde **800-279825,** attivo 24 ore su 24.

Per favore, guardi anche l'altra parte del foglio →

Front

1. Issuing office
2. Your name and address
3. Bill reference number
4. Period to which bill applies
5. ENEL reference code
6. Type of electricity supply
7. Maximum electricity power supply
8. Period being re-assessed
9. Last meter reading
10. Previous meter reading
11. Total consumption
12. Breakdown of estimated and actual consumption bi-monthly
13. Difference between estimated and actual consumption in total
14. Amount due is difference between estimated and actual consumption
15. Information regarding phoning in your meter readings

Fig. 8. The electricity bill.

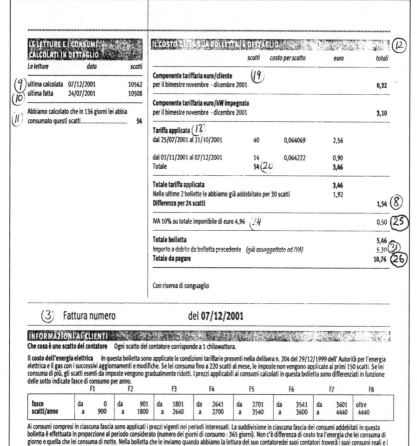

LE LETTURE E I CONSUMI CALCOLATI IN DETTAGLIO

Le letture	data	scatti
ultima calcolata	07/12/2001	10562
ultima fatta	24/07/2001	10508

Abbiamo calcolato che in 136 giorni lei abbia consumato questi scatti............................ 54

IL COSTO DELLA SUA BOLLETTA IN DETTAGLIO

	scatti	costo per scatto	euro	totali
Componente tariffaria euro/cliente per il bimestre novembre - dicembre 2001				0,32
Componente tariffaria euro/kW impegnato per il bimestre novembre - dicembre 2001				3,10
Tariffa applicata dal 25/07/2001 al 31/10/2001	40	0,064069	2,56	
dal 01/11/2001 al 07/12/2001	14	0,064222	0,90	
Totale	54		3,46	
Totale tariffa applicata			3,46	
Nelle ultime 2 bollette le abbiamo già addebitato per 30 scatti			1,92	
Differenza per 24 scatti				1,54
IVA 10% su totale imponibile di euro 4,96				0,50
Totale bolletta				5,46
Importo a debito da bolletta precedente *(già assoggettato ad IVA)*				5,30
Totale da pagare				10,76

Con riserva di conguaglio

(3) Fattura numero   del **07/12/2001**

INFORMAZIONI AI CLIENTI

Che cosa è uno scatto del contatore Ogni scatto del contatore corrisponde a 1 chilowattora.

Il costo dell'energia elettrica   In questa bolletta sono applicate le condizioni tariffarie presenti nella delibera n. 204 del 29/12/1999 dell' Autorità per l'energia elettrica e il gas con i successivi aggiornamenti e modifiche. Se lei consuma fino a 220 scatti al mese, le imposte non vengono applicate ai primi 150 scatti. Se lei consuma di più, gli scatti esenti da imposte vengono gradualmente ridotti. I prezzi applicabili ai consumi calcolati in questa bolletta sono differenziati in funzione delle sotto indicate fasce di consumo per anno.

	F1		F2		F3		F4		F5		F6		F7		F8
fasce scatti/anno	da a	0 900	da a	901 1800	da a	1801 2640	da a	2641 2700	da a	2701 3540	da a	3541 3600	da a	3601 4440	oltre 4440

Ai consumi compresi in ciascuna fascia sono applicati i prezzi vigenti nei periodi interessati. La suddivisione in ciascuna fascia dei consumi addebitati in questa bolletta è effettuata in proporzione al periodo considerato (numero dei giorni di consumo : 365 giorni). Non c'è differenza di costo tra l'energia che lei consuma di giorno e quella che lei consuma di notte. Nella bolletta che le inviamo quando abbiamo la lettura del suo contatore dei suoi contatori troverà i suoi consumi reali e i prezzi applicati per ciascun periodo tariffario.

Back

16. ENEL telephone number to use if phoning in meter reading
17. Customer number
18. Space to write down meter reading
19. Bi-monthly standing charge
20. Amount brought forward from 10
21. Customer number
22. Debit by standing order
23. Pay-by-date
24. Amount subject to IVA (VAT)
25. Amount of IVA (VAT) payable
26. Total payable
27. Bill reference number (As 3)
28. As 4
29. Fiscal code number
30. Returnable deposit taken for connection of electricity supply

The electricity bill continued.

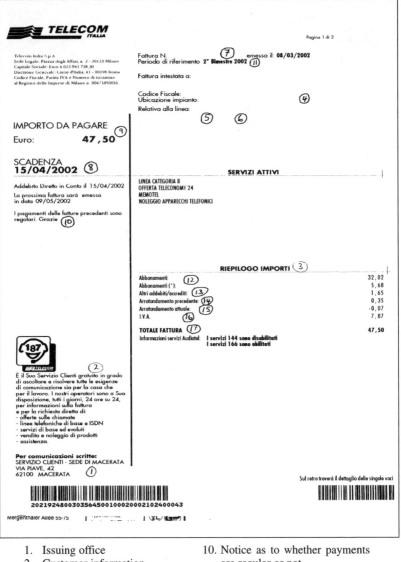

1. Issuing office
2. Customer information
3. Breakdown of the bill
4. Location of apparatus
5. Telephone code
6. Telephone number
7. Bill number (eg 6th bi-monthly bill of 92)
8. Pay-by-date
9. Amount
10. Notice as to whether payments are regular or not
11. Period during which points have been assessed
12. Standing charge
13. Other debits/credits
14. Rounding up of preceding bill
15. Rounding up of actual bill
16. VAT
17. Bill total

Fig. 9. The phone bill.

italgas Più

 SERVIZIO CLIENTI
Via G.Guicciardi, 53
00168 ROMA

③ Numero
Cliente:

ITALGAS Più S.p.A.
Sede Legale e D.F.Torino, Via XX Settembre 41
Cap. Soc. € 30.000.000 i.v.
R.I. Torino, Cod. Fisc. e P.IVA N. 08105000015

①

②

Riferimento fattura 20011111 emessa il 17/11/2001
(ex. art. 21 D.P.R. N. 633/72 IVA e art.1 D.M. 370 24/10/2000)

FATTURA PER LA FORNITURA DI GAS

Periodo:15 Marzo - 17 Novembre 2001 ⑤

Forniamo Gas a:

Le comunichiamo che, in attuazione
del Decreto Legislativo n.164
del 23/5/00, Italgas ha costituito
Italgas Più' S.p.A., società' alla
quale ha trasferito le attività
di vendita del gas. Pertanto, il Suo
contratto di fornitura gas proseguira',
alle medesime condizioni, con
Italgas Più' S.p.A.

Le sono stati addebitati
18 m³.
così' calcolati: ⑨

Lettura fattura precedente al ⑩
14/03/2001   2.059
Lettura ns. incaricato
08/11/2001   2.077
Lettura presunta al
17/11/2001   2.077

IL TOTALE DA PAGARE
E' DI EURO: ⑥

7,23
(Lire   14.000)

Pagata il ⑦

03/12/2001

s.b.f. su c/c
BANCA POPOLARE

NUMERI UTILI

Servizio Clienti:
  N.VERDE 800 900700

Servizio segnalazione guasti
e dispersioni:
  N.VERDE 800/900999

Servizio comunicazione letture:
  N.VERDE 800/999800

Servizio Clienti Internet:
  www.italgasclienti.it

⑪
Prossima fattura prevista:
23/03/2002.
Si presume che il contatore segnera'
Comunicando la lettura dal
17/03/2002 al 20/03/2002,
attraverso il N.Verde o il
Sito Internet a fianco in-
dicati, Le saranno addebitati i consumi corrispon-
denti alla lettura da Lei
trasmessa. Il servizio non
sostituisce la lettura
periodica del nostro incaricato.

1. Client name
2. Client address
3. Client reference number
4. Issuing office
5. Period of gas consumption
6. Total to pay
7. Date paid by direct debit
8. Bank details
9. Total consumed
10. Meter reading
11. Date next bill

Fig. 10. The gas bill.

the home although they are provided in most cafes. Probably the most popular newspapers are those dedicated to sports, the gutter press restricting itself to magazines. Most of the national papers tend to be of a similar standard and format, and frequently contain a local section. Local papers also exist in their own right. In Tuscany and Umbria there is *La Nazione* and *La Gazzetta*, in Emilia Romagna there is *Il Resto del Carlino*, in the Marches there is *Il Corriere Adriatico* and in Livorno there is *Il Tirreno*. These types of papers not only provide local news but usually have pages of classified advertisements and are the place to look if you are searching for a job. Local papers, and also local editions of the national papers, usually contain emergency telephone numbers, information on entertainment and local public transport.

DEALING WITH RED TAPE

Fulfilling any bureaucratic procedure in Italy is a time-consuming and often frustrating business. In the larger cities the problem is exacerbated by long queues and less than helpful staff. It is often difficult to make headway without the right personal contacts who can make things move, so many people take their problems to an agency, known as an **agenzia**, which specialises in dealing with bureaucratic formalities. As well as the correct documents almost any bureaucratic transaction requires *bolli* (state stamps), the most common type of which cost 7.75 Euros. and are purchased from *tabacchi* (tobacconists).

Police registration

Whether you are in Italy for a short-term or long-term stay you are required by law to register with the local police (either the *Questura*, or *Commissariato* or *Stazione di Carabinieri*) within three days of your arrival. If you are staying in a hotel, *pensione* or an approved campsite this formality will automatically be done for you.

Applying for a permit to stay

One of the first things you should do if you intend to stay in Italy for longer than 30 days is to apply for a *Permesso di Soggiorno* (Permit to Stay) within seven days of your arrival. Permits are issued by the *Ufficio Stranieri* (Foreign Department) or *Questura* of the Police in your regional capital, although the police in your local town may be willing to apply for the permit on your behalf. If you are applying through your local police station you will be required to write a formal letter of request accompanied by a *bollo* (state stamp). An example of the type of letter you should write is given below.

Alla Questura di (insert province)
(your name)

Il sottoscritto, nato/a (place of birth)
il (date of birth) *cittadino/a* (nationality)
in possesso di passaporto n. (passport number)
rilasciato il (date of issue) *e valido fino al* (expiry date)
rivolge corte domanda affinché gli/le venga l'autorizzazione per soggionare in Italia, (place), *per motivi di studio/lavoro/salute* (delete as applicable).
Allega:
(make a list of enclosures)
Il/la richiedente ha fatto ingresso in Italia il (date of entry into Italy) *tramite la frontiera di* (name of frontier crossed).

recapito all' estero: (date of return)
Inoltre' dichiara di abitare a (Italian address).

Con osservanza
Firma (legible signature)

The letter should be typed on special lined paper used for legal transactions, which has wide margins at either side. It is known as **carta uso bollo** and is available from *tabacchi* (tobacconists). Affix the correct *bolli* (state stamps) in the right-hand margin at the top of the page.

The type of permit you apply for will depend on your reason for being in Italy. However, you would normally be requested to present proof of your financial means or, where applicable, proof of your intended status *ie* student, worker, property owner, retired person, person of independent financial means.

Non-EU nationals wishing to apply to live permanently in Italy, for whatever reason, should contact the visa section of their local Italian Consulate.

Applying for residency

If you plan to take up residency in Italy, once you have obtained your *Permesso di Soggiorno* your next task is to register at the **Ufficio Anagrafe** (municipal registry office) in your nearest *Comune* or *Municipio* (town hall). Take your *Permesso di Soggiorno* and passport or identity card and explain that you wish to become a resident of the local *Comune*.

Once you are a resident you will find it much easier to do domestic transactions, such as opening a bank account, buying a car, having electricity connected *etc*, which require you to have a **Certificato di Residenza**.

To obtain this certificate simply go to the *Ufficio Anagrafe* where they will issue a print-out with the relevant information. The cost of the print-out is nominal, although most transactions require that a *bollo* is fixed to the certificate. If this is the case, buy it beforehand from the *tabacchi* (tobacconists) so that the *Ufficio Anagrafe* can put their official stamp on it.

Codice Fiscale

The **Codice Fiscale** is a card with your fiscal tax number on it. You will be asked to present this card for any number of transactions, from joining a club to opening a bank account. Registration is simple. Find out where your provincial tax office, known as **Ufficio Imposte Dirette**, is and present your passport or identity card. It will be issued there and then. Figure 11 shows an example of a *Codice Fiscale* card.

CAR AND DRIVER DOCUMENTATION

Obtaining an Italian driving licence

Foreigners resident in Italy are required by law to obtain an Italian driving licence within a year of the date on which they registered at their local *Comune* or *Municipio* (town hall). The procedure to do so is quite a lengthy one and you may prefer to avoid the whole rigmarole by buying an International Driving Licence which can be renewed each year.

However, those who want an Italian licence should read on. The first step is to have an Italian translation of your British

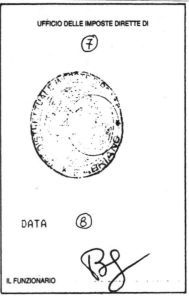

1. Fiscal code number
2. Surname
3. First name
4. Place of birth
5. Province of birth
6. Date of birth
7. Tax office
8. Date

Fig. 11. The *Codice Fiscale* card.

licence made. A standard translation for a European Union-type British Driving Licence is provided below. You should transfer this translation, filling in the appropriate data, onto the special lined paper with margins at either side, *carta uso bollo*, available from *tabacchi* (tobacconists). Do not write in either of the margins but in the right-hand one affix a *bollo* (state stamp), which is also available from *tabacchi*.

Dipartimento di trasporto (insert country)
Patente di guida, tipo (insert type)
Nome: (insert first names)
Cognome: (insert surname)
Date e luogo di nascita: (insert place and date of birth)
Domicilio: (insert address)
Rilasciato dal: (insert issuing office)
Il giorno: (insert date of issue)
Valido fino al (insert expiry date)
Patente (insert licence number)
Autorizzata a guidare tipo (insert code for type of vehicles authorised to drive) *soltanto i moto veicoli tipo* (insert code for authorised vehicles) *se il conducente ha l'eta per guidare. Vedere il regolamento minimo eta per guidare che e nella parte posteriore.*

A 18 anni: Motoveicoli con il massimo portata di peso non superiore a 7.5 Ton. Altri moto veicoli autorizzati di merce. Grande veicolo per passegeri in concomitanza con la regole No. 4 del motoveicoli (Licenza di guida). Regolamenti 1987. Vedere trasporto merce pesante e veicoli de trasporto pubblico. A 21 anni: Motoveicoli grandi per passegeri, con il massimo peso piu di 7.5 Ton. Altri veicoli non elencati sopra. Vedere Guida di merce pesante e Veicoli di Servizio

*Pubblico. I summenzionati limiti di eta non saranno appli-
cati per i veicoli del gruppo A, B, G, H, K, L e N quando
sono per uso Navale Militare ossia per motivi di Forze Aero.*

*Per guidare veicolo per merce pesante e veicoli di Servizio
Pubblico: Devi ottenere una licenza supplementare prima
di guidare sia un veicolo pesante o veicolo de servizio
pubblico.*

*Veicolo grande per passegeri, si intende un veicolo a posita-
mente costruito ossia trasportare piu di 9 persone compreso
il conducente. Veicoli per merce: si intende un veicolo, eccetto moto veicolo grande per passegeri o pure trattori per agricoltura, costruito o adattato per trasportare tirare e con il
massimo peso eccedente 3.5 Ton. Il massimo peso e il peso
massimo quando il veicolo potrebbe pesare a pieno carico;
comprende il peso de qualunque rimorchio o semi rimorchio.
Elenco di tipo di licenze per guidare:*

*A. Qualunque veicoli eccetto veicoli gruppo D (Moto
veicoli), tipo E (Ciclomotore), tipo G (rullo compressore),
tipo H (cingolato caterpillar), tipo J (veicoli per invalidi)
E. Ciclomotore di 50CC*

La sudetta patente porta un numero ad ogni margine (insert
code numbers printed on edges of licence).

Once you have completed the translation you must take it to
your local **Pretura or Tribunale** (Magistrate's Court) and
have it stamped and signed by the appropriate clerk. Next
you should go to the *Comune* or *Municipio* (town hall) with
a *bollo* (state stamp) and three passport-sized photographs.

Ask the *Ufficio Anagrafe* in your local *Comune* or *Municipio* for a *Certificato di Residenza* (Resident's Certificate) and have the *bollo* attached and stamped. Also ask someone in the *Comune* or *Municipio* to authenticate one of your photographs, verifying that it is a true likeness.

Then make arrangements for a **Certificato Medico** (Medical Certificate). First you must obtain a medical report form and a blank medical certificate. These are usually available either from an *agenzia* who deals with licence exchange (look for *patente* written in their window), or from your *Unita Sanataria Locale* (USL). Take the medical report form to your family doctor to fill in and sign. Next take the report, along with the blank medical certificate, a *bollo* and a pass-port-sized photograph to the *Unita Sanitaria Locale* (USL). Here you will be given an eye test, after which you will be issued with the final medical certificate.

Having done all this, gather together every single scrap of relevant paper, as well as your current driving licence, and head either to a *Motorirazzione Civile* office, the address of which can be found by looking in the *Pagine Gialle* (Yellow Pages) under *Ministero del Trasporto*, or delegate the task to the Automobile Club Italiano (ACI) or an *agenzia* (agent). At this stage of the proceedings you will be asked to hand over your original driving licence and a photocopy of it. It will be some days before your Italian licence is ready, therefore remember to ask for a letter or some proof that you hold a licence, in case you should be stopped by the police in the meantime. If you decide to go to the *Motorirazzione Civile* yourself, you will be asked to pay a postal order at the post office and to purchase another *bollo*. Checklist of documents for obtaining an Italian Driving Licence:

- Italian translation of British licence with a state stamp and signature of magistrate's court

- photocopy of original driving licence

- Residence Certificate with a state stamp

- three photographs (one to be endorsed by the town hall)

- medical certificate with a state stamp.

A facsimile of an Italian driving licence is shown in Figure 12.

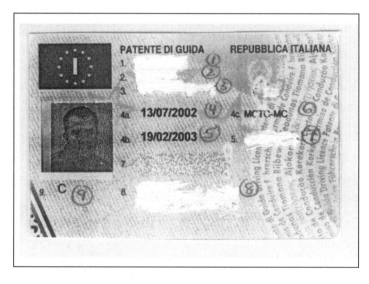

1. Surname
2. First name
3. Date/place of birth
4. Date of issue
5. Date of expiry

6. Issuing office
7. Licence number
8. Address
9. Category

Fig. 12. The Italian driving licence.

Importing and registering a foreign car

If you are a registered resident in Italy and have a foreign-registered vehicle you are obliged to import it and obtain Italian number plates. The procedure involved in doing this is extremely long, complicated and expensive, so if possible don't attempt it. If you have no alternative then you are well advised to use your local Automobile Club Italiano (ACI) representative to help you, although if you are living in a rural backwater you may find that the ACI office know less about the procedure than you.

The first stage in the process is to complete the importation formalities. This means that your V561 export certificate must be stamped by customs and must show any tax or duty that was paid. If you did not have this done on crossing the border you should go to your nearest customs office.

The next stage is to locate your local *Motorirazzione Civile* office, which can found by looking in the *Pagine Gialle* (Yellow Pages) under *Ministero del Trasporto*, and take along the following documents:

- V561 Export Certificate paid and stamped
- Technical Data Certificate
- authenticated translation of Technical Data Certificate
- Residence Certificate
- *Domanda in Carta Semplice.*

The Residence Certificate is available from your local *Comune* or *Municipio*. The *Domanda* is a formal, typed letter on plain paper requesting the matriculation of your vehicle. A model letter is shown below:

Motorirazzione Civile
Address

Date

La sottoscritto/a (name), *nato/a il* (date of birth), *a* (place and country of birth), *richiede la vista e prova per effetuare la nazionalizzazione della sua autovettura* (make and model of vehicle)
Numero Motore: (engine number)
Numero Targa: (numberplate)

in fede

(Date) (Signature)

When you present yourself to the *Motorirazzione Civile* office you will be given a form, the *Domanda di Vista e Prova per Immatricolazione* (Request for Inspection and Test for Matriculation) Model number MC2102MEC. This must be completed with all your details and the appropriate postal orders paid at a post office.

The next stage is for the *Motorirazzione Civile* to administer an inspection and test to check that your vehicle conforms to Italian standards.

Provided the vehicle passes the test you are now eligible for Italian plates. On collection of your plates you will be presented with a bill which will probably include the cost of the plates, the cost of the vehicle inspection and a fee paid to the lawyer who verified your new matriculation papers. On top of this you will pay IVA (VAT) of 20 per cent. You shouldn't be surprised by a bill in excess of 500 Euros, and of course if you used an agent it will also include their fee. Your matriculation papers will be sent through the post. In the meantime you should be given a provisional document which covers you for one month.

Finding Accommodation

HOLIDAY ACCOMMODATION

Hotels and pensione

Italian hotels are classified under a five-star rating scheme, although the corresponding tariffs vary greatly. Prices are in general high by European standards; a single room in a one-star hotel or a *pensione* can easily set you back 25 Euros. Your bill will include IVA (VAT) of 20 per cent.

If you want to book hotel accommodation before arriving in Italy you can contact a travel agent or a hotel representative. A comprehensive list of hotel representatives in the UK can be obtained from the Italian State Tourist Office (see Appendix for address). However, travel agents and hotel representatives generally only deal with four- or five-star hotels. Otherwise, it is of course possible to phone a hotel directly.

Holiday villages

Many Italians spend their summer vacation in a *villaggio turistico,* a holiday village, which is a self-contained complex often sited on the coast near a holiday resort, with a variety of facilities for sport and leisure as well as restaurants, shops and bars. The accommodation is self-catering, making it a very popular option for families. Bookings should be made well in advance for the months of July and August.

Agriturismo

Agriturismo is an organisation that offers vacations in rural locations, often in Italian family homes. The great majority of Agriturismo accommodation is concentrated in Trentino Alto Adige, Tuscany and Umbria, and more recently in Sardinia. The type of accommodation varies considerably, from being a very basic bed and breakfast to a plush country hotel with excursions arranged and sports facilities available. At the lower end of the range, you can expect to pay considerably less than you would for a hotel, but you may be expected to offer some work in exchange. In some Agriturismo establishments you can specify the type of lodging you want: whether it is *per nottamento e prima colazione* (bed and breakfast) or *mezza pensione* (half-board). You may find there is a special offer for a *weekend completo* (full weekend) which includes the Friday evening meal and Sunday lunch. Most Agriturismo lodgings are affiliated to a regional organisation which determines the tariffs. To find out more about Agriturismo holidays request the *Guida dell'Ospitalita Rurale* from this address:

Agriturist Centro Prenotazioni
Via di Monte Brianzo
00186 Roma
Tel: 06 6875563
  Or search the full guide at www.agriturismo.net

For individual Agriturismo destinations consult Pagine Gialle online at www.paginegialle.com. Alternatively search www.turismoverde.com.

Campsites

There are some 2,000 campsites dotted along Italy's coasts.

They are classified into four categories and are priced accordingly, although the figures vary from district to district. Your bill will consist of a fee charged per person, a fee for the pitch, a charge for electricity, IVA (VAT) and usually a tourist tax. Children under three are generally not charged. Members of AIT or FICC or FIA are offered discounts.

Most campsites are open from April until September or October. However, those in the mountainous northern regions do not open until June, while some sites in the warmer south stay open all year round.

For a comprehensive listing and prices of campsites in Italy contact Federcampeggio which publishes a free guide called *Campeggi in Italian*.

Federcampeggio
Casella Postale 23
Via Vittorio Emanuele 11
Calenzano
Florence
Tel: (055) 882391.

Information on availability of space in campsites can be obtained from offices of the Automobile Club Italiano (ACI), and from provincial tourist offices known as Ente Provinciale del Turismo.

Alternatively try www.initaly.com or www.camping.it

Youth hostels

Youth hostels are not very widespread in Italy; there are little over 50 in total and the rates often exceed those of the lowest category *pensione*. To stay at a hostel you must have a membership card issued by the International Youth Hostel Federation (IYHF). If you do not already have one it can be purchased at the youth hostel itself, an authorised travel agency, a Youth Information Centre (see Appendix for addresses) or from a centre of Associazione Italiana Alberghi per la Gioventu, the head office of which is given below:

Associazione Italiana Alberghi per la Gioventu
Via Cavour 44
00184 Roma
Tel: 06 4871152.
www.travel.it/hostels

FINDING LONG-TERM ACCOMMODATION

Doing a house exchange

Exchanging your UK home for an Italian one, either permanently or for a specified period, is a good way of solving the accommodation problem, although it is important that the conditions and securities are clearly laid out.

Try www.homeexchange.com or www.homebase-hols.com

Finding rented accommodation

Finding a place to rent is fairly difficult in most towns and cities throughout Italy. Houses are particularly hard to come by; most people rent flats. Added to the scarce availability, rents tend to be very high. To rent a two-bedroom flat in Florence, for example, costs anything from 775 Euros per month, and this is exclusive of service charges and running costs. The scarcity and high cost of rented accommodation is a direct result of a fair rent act that was passed in 1978, known as the *Legge dell 'Equo Canone'*. The act states that the minimum lease is for four years and that the rent must conform to the rates fixed by the law. The rates are calculated according to the land registry classification and the standard of the accommodation.To find a place to rent you can:

- go to a housing agency (many agencies are only concerned with the sale and purchase of property)
- consult the local tourist office
- look in the local papers
- ask around locally
- walk the streets in the area in which you plan to live looking for *affitasi* or *da affitare* (to rent) signs posted on front doors.

Once you have found a place you will have to negotiate terms, and it may be in your interest to offer to pay in undeclared cash in return for a lower rent. The landlord can ask for a deposit of up to the value of three months' rent.

If you are renting a flat in an apartment block with more than five proprietors you will be liable for joint service charges. These include such things as air conditioning, cleaning services and lift maintenance and are arranged by a joint owners' assembly, known as a *condominio*. The service charges also usually encompass the cost of central heating which is run off a communal boiler. Italy has official heating times, running from October to April, which means that boilers in apartment blocks are not lit outside these times. If you wish to contest any of the service charges or facilities, the assembly will put your issue to the vote.

You may be interested to know that once you are settled in a rented flat you cannot be legally evicted except by court order. Harassment of tenants is also illegal.

BUYING A PROPERTY

In Italy properties for sale are dealt with by *agenzie immobiliare* (estate agents). Many are franchises, such as Grimaldi, and FIAIP registered.

The system tends to be for you to describe the type of property you are looking for, and name your price bracket. The local *agenzie* is best consulted when you are looking for regular modern housing. If you are looking for a property to renovate or one that is ready-restored, British agencies usually advertise in the property columns of the British Sunday newspapers.

Other ways of finding property if you are already in Italy include searching through the classified advertisements in local newspapers and also in the monthly property journal, *Metroquadro*, which can be subscribed by contacting the following address:

Metroquadro
Via Madonna Della Querce 8
50133 Firenze
Tel: 055 577404

Alternatively consult the local town hall *comune*, in the area that you are looking for property.

Once you have found a property you will need to contact a *notaio* (notary), the public official responsible for drawing up the deeds (*rogito*) and registering the transfer of property. They are listed in the *Pagine Gialle* (Yellow Pages) under *Notai*.

The first step in the buying process is for the *notaio* to make searches into the ownership of the property in question, in order to ensure legitimacy of the seller and to check that there is no mortgage or other payment outstanding. At the same time a *geometra* should be employed to carry out a survey, and it is necessary to open a bank account.

The next step is to go ahead with the preliminary contract, the *compromesso*. While this is being drawn up you should obtain a *Codice Fiscale*, an Italian Fiscal Code number, which will need to be presented at all further meetings with the *notaio* (as well as a passport and identity card). The purpose of the *compromesso* is to clarify all conditions of the sale, including the price and terms of payment. This stage involves the payment of a deposit of between 10 and 30 per cent of the sale price of the property.

The normal procedure after signing the *compromesso* is to meet again in the presence of the *notaio* on the completion date to exchange contracts, a procedure known as the *atto*. The *notaio* should have rechecked the ownership of the property and any outstanding payments and have drawn up the title deed, the *rogito*. The *notaio* reads out the final contract and then certifies the signatures of the buyer and seller. Finally he asks the buyer to pay the fees incurred and also any taxes that are due. Once the purchase price has been paid to the seller, monies transferred and the title deed is signed, the property has officially changed hands. The *notaio* then has to register the title deed at the *cadastro* (land registry), and your copy of the certified title deed will be ready for collection or delivery after about two months.

6

Health and Welfare

WORKING OUT THE HEALTH SYSTEM

Public health care

The Italian public health system, the *Servizio Sanitario Nazionale* (SSN), is administered by local health departments known as *Unita Sanitaria Locale* (USL). There are approximately 650 USL health departments in Italy, each of which serves between 50,000 and 200,000 inhabitants. Depending on the size of the local population, a health department caters for a single *comune* (commune), or an association of smaller *comuni* (communes), or a *comunita montana* (mountain community). To locate your local USL look in the telephone directory under *Unita Sanitaria Locale*. Register with your nearest USL to obtain a national health number. Thereafter you can register with a local general practitioner (*medico convenzionato*) – a list is generally obtainable from your local USL.

USL (pronounced 'oosle'), as well as being an administrative body, provides public health services too. There is usually a rotation of doctors and specialists on duty, the hours of which can be found posted on a bulletin board inside the building. Doctors and specialists who are *con la mutua* (under the SSN) operate part-time *ambulatorio* (consulting rooms) at hospitals too. There will be a noticeboard posted inside the hospital showing the hours. Doctors and specialists who work under the SSN also have their own surgeries, the addresses of which can be found out from your local USL centre.

In addition, the State provides counselling, family planning and paediatric care at local health units, known as *consultorio* (consultancy). A *consultorio* varies from place to place, but it invariably endeavours to serve the needs of the community in matters that are not dealt with by USL or otherwise. To locate your local *consultorio* (consultancy) look in the telephone directory, or if you live in a very small community enquire at USL or your local *municipio* or *comune* (town hall).

EU nationals who are unemployed and looking for work are also entitled to register with the Italian health service (Servizio Sanitario Nazionale or SSN) upon presentation of their *tesserino di disoccupazione* (unemployment registration card).

Private health care

The private health system in Italy is well used and quite extensive, ranging from small private practices to large private hospitals. Private health care offers the obvious advantages of avoiding long waiting lists for operations, and provides the extra care and comfort that may not be available in state institutions. Italians are usually covered by *mutua* or an insurance scheme that enables them to use the private health system.

Without any such cover, the costs involved in private health care are considerable. If you use a private doctor, you can expect to pay an initial registration fee and then the cost of each visit.

Dental care

Dentists in Italy are virtually all privately run. A small and overworked number belong to the public health scheme, but they do not have a good reputation and getting an appointment can be difficult. However, private dental care in Italy is no more expensive than in the UK and treatment is generally of a high standard. It is also worth remembering that if you are making a tax declaration in Italy you can offset any dentistry receipts against your taxable income.

How do you join the public health system?

In order to be eligible for public health care in Italy you must either have form E111 (see Chapter 2) or pay the obligatory health tax imposed by INPS, payable annually, which provides maternity and sickness benefits as well as health assistance. If you have an Italian employer, health tax payments will probably be made on your behalf. The employer is usually responsible for paying the greater part of the contributions while the remainder is automatically deducted from the employee's salary. If you are self-employed or unemployed you must make contributions by applying to your local tax office in person.

How contributions are assessed

The contributions are assessed according to a person's salary. If husband and wife both work they are assessed separately. If there is only one wage earner in the family then their contribution will cover any dependants. Those with salaries of up to 20,600 Euros pay 5 per cent, while for those that earn between 20,600 and 51,650 Euros, 4 per cent is deducted. If your taxable income is derived from land, property or capital the first 2,060 Euros of your income is exempt.

A problem for newcomers to the system is that the contributions are calculated according to the salary that is shown on your *denuncia* (income tax return) of the preceding year. If you have not made a tax declaration then you will be asked to pay the minimum fixed rate of 387 Euros. In order to make this voluntary contribution you will have to present your *Attesta di Iscrizione* (Registration Card) from the *Ufficio di Collocamento* (employment office), or if you are employed you must take a statement from your employer to prove that you are working.

Registering with the SSN

All residents in Italy, even if they are temporary or only use the private health sector, are obliged to register under the SSN. Enrolment runs out on 31 December of every year and you must go to USL in person to renew it.

In order to register, foreign residents should take the following documents to their local USL centre:

- an official identity document (driver's licence, passport, *etc.*)
- *stato di famiglia* (family status certificate)
- *certificato di residenza* (residence certificate) (both above available from *Ufficio Anagrafe*)
- *codice fiscale* (fiscal code card)
- letter from employer stating work situation, and a statement by INPS that you are regularly employed, or
- *attesta di iscrizione* (registration card) from unemployment office
- *permesso di soggiorno* (permit to stay).

If you are registering as a temporary resident then you should submit your E111 in return for a certificate of entitlement. If you do not have an E111 you may be asked to provide some document that indicates your reason for staying in Italy. If you are working as an au pair, the family with whom you are living should present a request for enrolment within ten days of arrival. They must make an annual payment when they enrol.

When you register you will be asked to select from an approved list a family doctor and, in the case of children under the age of six, a paediatrician. Unless you have a personal recommendation choosing a doctor can be difficult. You may wish to consider the location of the surgery and parking availability, the opening hours, whether they speak any English and whether they have an appointment system. USL will probably not be able to answer these questions, but if you take the doctors' telephone numbers you can ring them and find out for yourself. If you find that you do not get on with your doctor you can transfer by informing USL.

After completing the registration formalities at USL you will be given a temporary cover note which lasts until your *tessera sanitaria* (health card) arrives in the post. A separate health card is issued for each member of your family. The *tessera sanitaria* (health card) is a vital document, bearing your fiscal code number, and should be carried on you whenever you need medical care. If you should lose your card then apply to USL without delay for a duplicate. The *tessera* is valid for one year only. Each time you renew it you should take all the documents that were listed for your initial registration as above. A facsimile of a *tessera sanitaria* is shown in Figure 13.

USING THE PUBLIC HEALTH SYSTEM

Family doctors

The touchstone in the health system, both public and private, is the family doctor with whom you enlist when you register at USL. Whether you have a dose of flu, an ingrown toe-nail, or need a medical certificate for work, your family doctor is the person to see.

The first thing to do is to find out the hours that your doctor works. Although proposals have been put forward to change the way surgeries are run, it is still generally the case that each doctor has his own small surgery which only operates for limited hours. It is seldom possible to make an appointment, surgeries usually operate on a first-come-first-served basis. Patients sort this out amongst themselves using a form of Pelmanism, there generally being no secretary or receptionist. Allow plenty of time.

Inside the doctor's room there is no fear of any rigorous medical examination; pen and paper are the family doctor's instruments. The role of the family doctor is to diagnose a problem and then to write out the appropriate *impegnativa*, which is a chit that either serves to take your problem elsewhere or prescribes drugs to be purchased at the chemist. (See facsimile of *impegnativa* in Figure 14.)

Paediatricians

Italian children up to the age of 14 usually go to a paediatrician rather than the family doctor. They operate in the same way as family doctors, having their own surgeries and working within restricted hours. They write out an *impegnativa* (chit) as and when necessary, but generally problems are solved within the surgery. The paediatrician also gives routine check-ups and advises on children's diet.

What to do in emergencies

If you need medical assistance outside surgery hours go to the *pronto soccorso* (first aid) department at the nearest hospital. Alternatively, call the district duty doctor, whose number can be found in the telephone directory under *guardia medica*, or dial one of the national emergency numbers, either 112 or 113.

In tourist areas, during the holiday season, there is usually a *guardia medica turistica*, a doctor who speaks at least one foreign language. The *guardia medica turistica* operates in the same way as a family doctor, as well as providing emergency assistance.

Getting medical treatment

With an *impegnativa* (chit) in hand, the next stage in the game is to get the medical attention you require. To see a specialist, who will probably work within a state hospital or an USL building (local health unit), telephone beforehand to make an appointment or to find out working hours. When you arrive at the hospital or USL building hand over your *impegnativa* to the cashier and pay the *tickets*, which is the

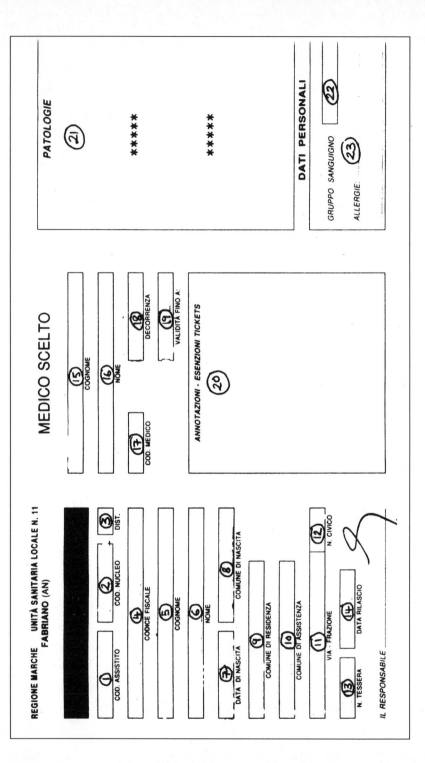

1. Assistance number
2. Unit number
3. District
4. Fiscal code number
5. Surname
6. First name
7. Date of birth
8. Place of birth
9. Municipality of residence
10. Municipality of assistance
11. Street (address)
12. Number (address)
13. Number of medical card
14. Date of issue
15. Surname of doctor
16. Name of doctor
17. Doctor's code number
18. Date valid from
19. Date valid until
20. Notes – Exemptions from *tickets* (charges)
21. Medical
22. Blood group
23. Allergies

Fig. 13. *Tessera sanitaria*: medical card.

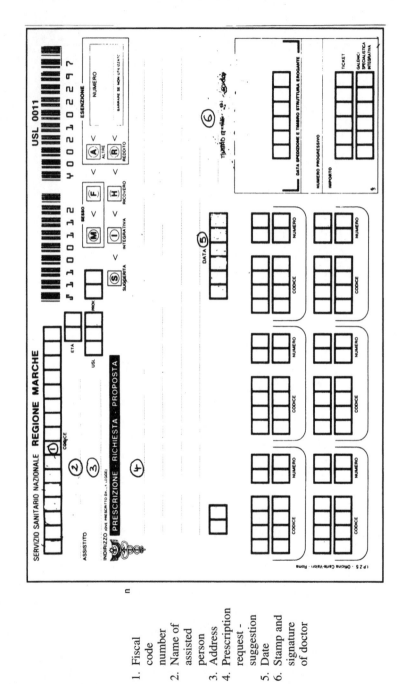

Fig. 14. A doctor's *impegnativa*.

1. Fiscal code number
2. Name of assisted person
3. Address
4. Prescription request - suggestion
5. Date
6. Stamp and signature of doctor

subsidised charge. In return you will be given a receipt to be taken to the relevant specialist. If your *impegnativa* is to get a laboratory test or an X-ray done, you are responsible for collecting the results and taking them back to the doctor to read. So make sure you know when and how the results are available and don't lose them!

Medical costs

If you pay state health tax you will pay subsidised charges, known as *tickets*, for specialist visits, prescribed medicines, hospital treatment, X-rays and laboratory tests. The amount of subsidy depends on your family income level.

You will pay the full amount for prescriptions up to 13 Euros and then ten per cent of any additional cost. You also pay the full cost for specialist visits and laboratory tests up to 52 Euros and then ten per cent of any amount in excess.

Services that are free of charge for all citizens under the SSN (National Health Service) include:

- visits to the family doctor or paediatrician
- all treatment related to pregnancy (including abortion)
- emergency hospital treatment
- the services at a *consultorio* (local health unit)
- emergency ambulance services (see below).

You are eligible for further health subsidies, such as exemption from the payment of *tickets*, if your family income falls below 8,264 Euros per annum. In order to find out further information consult your local USL. You will need to take proof of your income, preferably in the form of the previous year's tax declaration, or if applicable information regarding your pension or other benefit.

If you are going to make a tax declaration in Italy you should keep all receipts for medical treatment as they can be offset against your taxable income. You should also keep all medical receipts in order to make an insurance claim. This may also apply to holders of the E111 who were unable to obtain a certificate of entitlement from USL and who wish to apply for a reimbursement. Remember that medical costs include both treatment and drugs, so keep the official price tags that are attached to all medicines sold in Italian pharmacies, as well as medical bills.

Ambulances

In emergency situations you can call your family doctor for a house call or the doctor on emergency call, but during the night or at holidays it may be necessary to call an ambulance to take the ill person to the emergency room of a hospital. The various USL have their own rules about ambulance services. The following are some common types of regulations:

● emergency first aid ambulance: service is generally free of charge or else the ambulance service is reimbursed by the USL
● ambulance requested by the doctor on emergency call: generally free of charge or reimbursed by the USL
● hospital request for transportation of the patient to another hospital: free of charge to the patient (the hospital pays the charges)

- ambulance service requested by the patient (for example, for transportation home or to a private clinic): expenses charged to the patient.

WORKING OUT THE WELFARE SYSTEM

Maternity benefit

If you have been making regular INPS (welfare) contributions you should be paid maternity benefit. In order to obtain benefit apply to your local INPS office, taking with you a medical certificate confirming your pregnancy and a statement from your employer (if applicable) certifying that you have stopped work due to pregnancy. As soon as the child is born INPS expect to receive the child's birth certificate and a **stato di famiglia** (family status certificate), both of which are available from the *Ufficio Anagrafe* at your local *comune* or *municipio* (town hall).

Maternity benefit is paid for the two months preceding the expected delivery date and for the three months that follow. For women in regular employment, it is obligatory to take leave from work during this period. The benefit amounts to 80 per cent of your average daily earnings. You are also entitled to maternity benefit for six months during the year after the child is born. This allowance, however, only amounts to 30 per cent of your calculated daily earnings. If for any reason you cannot get maternity allowance in Italy, but you were last insured under the UK scheme you may get UK Maternity Allowance instead. Apply to the Benefits Agency for further information.

Sickness benefit

If you want to claim sickness benefit, send a medical certificate, stating the diagnosis and the period of incapacity for work, to your local INPS office. Benefit is only calculated after the INPS office receives the certificate so do not delay its delivery. If your illness continues beyond the date indicated on the certificate, send another certificate stating that you are still ill within two days of the original one expiring.

Sickness benefit is payable for a maximum of 180 days. The amount is calculated by assessing your average daily earnings in the month preceding your illness. You can expect to receive approximately 50 per cent of this amount. If your illness lasts for more than 21 days the amount is increased to two-thirds of your average daily earnings. If you are hospitalised and do not have dependants your allowance is reduced to two-fifths of your average daily earnings.

Family allowance

If you are the sole wage earner in your family, and you work for an employer or you are a farmer, a sharecropper or a farm-hand and your salary falls below a certain level you may apply for family allowance. Submit the application form, which is available either from your employer or an INPS office, along with a *stato di famiglia* (family status certificate) from your local *comune* (town hall), to your employer. The allowance will be paid by your employer at the same time as your salary.

Pensions

All employed people, and certain categories of self-employed people such as smallholders, sharecroppers and tenant farmers, craftsmen and tradespeople, are entitled to a pension from INPS. Other self-employed people who are pursuing a liberal profession, such as doctors, receive pensions through a separate organisation, the principal addresses of which are supplied below.

Ente Nazionale di Previdenza ed Assistenza Medici
  (ENPAM)
(National Welfare and Assistance Office for Medical
  Practitioners)
Via Sansotta Domenico 97
00144 Roma
Tel: 06 52207046

Ente Nazionale di Previdenza ed Assistenza per gli
  Psicologi
(National Welfare and Assistance Office for Psychologists)
Via Degli Scialoja 3
00196 Roma
Tel: 06 3230976

Ente Nazionale di Previdenza ed Assistenza Farmacisti
  (ENPAF)
(National Welfare and Assistance Office for Pharmacists)
Viale Pasteur 49
00144 Roma
Tel: 06 54711

Inarcassa Cassa Nazionale Previdenza Assistenza Ingg.
  Arch. Liberi Professionisti
(National Welfare Fund for Engineers and Architects)

Via Salaria 229
00199 Roma
Tel: 06 852741

Cassa Nazionale di Previdenza ed Assistenza a Favore di
   Dottori Commercialisti
(National Welfare and Assistance Fund for Economists)
Via Purificazione 31
00187 Roma
Tel: 06 42017902

Cassa Nazionale di Previdenza ed Assistenza a Favore di
   Ragioneri e Periti Commerciali
(National Welfare and Assistance Fund for Accountants)
Via Pollio Albertio 40
00159 Roma
Tel: 06 4385302

Ente Nazionale di Previdenza ed Assistenza per i
   Consulenti del Lavoro (ENPACL)
(National Welfare and Assistance Office for Employment
   Experts)
Viale Caravaggio 78
00147 Roma
Tel: 06 510541

Cassa Nazionale Notariato Centralino
(National Fund for Notaries)
Via Flaminia 160/162
00196 Roma
Tel: 06 369851

There are two types of pension paid in Italy. The first is a *Pensione di Anzianita*, a Seniority Pension, which is paid regardless of age provided that you have paid contributions for at least 35 years and have ceased working. The second is the *Pensione di Vecchiaia*, Old Age Pension, which is obtainable at the age of 55 for women and 60 for men. If you are self-employed the pensionable age is 60 for women and 65 for men. In order to be eligible for an old age pension you must have paid contributions for at least 15 years. Pensions are paid on the first day of the month following your application, which should be made to your local INPS office. The amount is calculated according to the number of years in which contributions were paid and your average earnings in the five years preceding your pension application. The maximum pension for a worker who has paid contributions for 40 years amounts to 80 per cent of the highest average annual income received during the preceding five years.

Lodging an appeal

If you do not agree with a decision that has been taken regarding your health and welfare situation you may appeal to the following institutions:

- INPS *Comitato Provinciale* (Provincial Committee)
- INPS *Comitato Speciale* (Special Committee)
- INPS *Comitato Regionale* (Regional Committee)
- *Ministero del Lavoro e della Sicurezza Sociale* (Ministry of Labour and Social Security).

If your appeal is not successful and you wish to take the matter further you may take your case to the ordinary courts of law.

OTHER HEALTH AND WELFARE CONCERNS

Drugs and alcohol

Drug abuse is widespread in Italy, perhaps not surprisingly since it is the second largest drug market in the world after the US, and drugs are comparatively cheap. However, the law is strict on prohibition and lifetime prison sentences are given to anyone found dealing in drugs.

Alcohol is less of a problem in Italy. The absence of pubs as social gathering places eliminates the beer lout, and Italian *ragazzi* (young people) tend to chat in the piazza over an ice-cream rather than an alcoholic drink. Having said this the alcohol consumption per capita is high, but this is because virtually all Italians drink wine with both lunch and dinner — and as many families have their own vineyard there are copious amounts to drink at very little cost.

The Association of Alcoholics Anonymous (Associazione Alcolisti Anonimi) has branches throughout Italy. Further information can be obtained from the head office:

Alcolisti Anonimi
Via Napoli 58
Rome
Tel: 06 4742913

Facilities for disabled travellers

Most Italian towns and cities, with their narrow cobbled streets and flights of stone stairs, are not very easily accessible to disabled travellers. Special facilities are rather few and far between. You will, however, find bathrooms for the disabled at all motorway service stations, in hospitals and usually at major tourist sights. You are well advised to plan your trip carefully, writing well in advance to the relevant tourist offices to find out exactly what facilities are available.

If you are travelling by car you must display your orange badge to use the reserved parking places that exist in most towns. If you plan to travel by train you will find that wheelchairs are taken free of charge. Special services are generally provided at airports, but it is important to specify your handicap beforehand.

For further information on travelling in Italy, contact the following address in the UK:

Radar
25 Mortimer Street
London W1M 8AB
Tel: 020 7250 3222

Head offices of some organisations in Italy that you may wish to contact are:

Associazione Italiana Assistenza Spastici (Italian
    Association for Assistance to Spastics) AIAS
Via Cipro 4/H
Rome 00136
Tel: 06 39731704

and

AIAS
Via S. Barnaba 29
Milan
Tel: 02 55017564

Unione Italiana dei Ciechi
(Italian Union for the Blind)
Via Monti E Tognetti 6
Monza 20052
Tel: 03 9382254.

Ente Nazionale Protezione e Assistenza Sordomuti
(National Corporation for the Protection and Assistance of
the Deaf and Dumb)
Via Gregorio VII 120
Rome 00165
Tel: 06 6380936.

Facilities for childcare

Childcare facilities for the under-threes, generally creches
(known as *nido*), are available in most towns and cities
throughout Italy. Childcare facilities at places of work are as
yet undeveloped and only exist in the large, industrial
Northern cities. If you want to employ a child-minder, ask
around locally or place an advertisement in a local shop or
newspaper. You will probably find that middle-aged women
who have just started to receive a state pension are the most
likely candidates. For children above the age of three see
Chapter 8, page 150.

$$\left(7 \right)$$

The Italian Job

JOB OPPORTUNITIES

Employment opportunities in Italy are open to all EU citizens. However, in order to be considered for a job in Italy you must either be equal to Italian nationals in language and training, or have an exclusive ability to offer. If you work in Italy you are entitled to exactly the same terms and conditions as Italian employees. Likewise, members of your family are entitled to the same benefits as members of an Italian employee's family.

Non-EU members will find getting a job in Italy more difficult. Vacancies are only given to non-EU members if there are no Italians suitable for the job. It is also necessary to apply for an **Entry Visa for Reasons of Work** (*visto d'ingresso per motivi di lavoro*) before arriving in Italy. This means that you must have a job arranged beforehand. In order to obtain a work visa send the contract with your employer's signature to the *Ufficio Provinciale del Lavoro* (Provincial Labour Office) and to the *Ufficio Stranieri* (Foreigners' Division) of the *Questura* (Provincial Police Headquarters). If you intend to work as a self-employed person in Italy contact the Italian Embassy or Consulate in your home country. You will also need a resident's permit and a special visa.

If you are a non-EU citizen coming to Italy for reasons other than work, but wish to take up employment after arriving, you must either be a foreign man married to an Italian woman or be a female Italian who changed nationality through marriage.

In July 2001, the National Statistics Bureau (www.istat.it) announced the Italian unemployment rate to have dropped slowly but surely from 11.4% to a miraculous 9.2%. There has been considerable debate and scepticism about how this figure was reached and the growth in the economy is said to reflect the introduction of more flexible work contracts – especially in the professional sector and service industries. Competition for work remains high and you should not come to Italy with false expectations. You should also remember that if by the time your temporary permit to stay has expired you have still not found a job, the police can charge you with vagrancy and escort you to the nearest border.

Looking for a job

If you are a resident in Italy and are looking for a job the first thing to do is to report to the police station, informing them that you are seeking employment. Next go to the *Ufficio Stranieri* (Foreigners' Division) of the provincial police headquarters and apply for a three-month *Permesso di Soggiorno* (see Chapter 4) which will permit you to stay in Italy while looking for work. The next task is to obtain a *Libretto di Lavoro* (Employment Book) by taking your *Permesso di Soggiorno* (Permit to Stay) to the *Comune* or *Municipio* (town hall) where you are registered as a resident. Then take the *Libretto di Lavoro* (which is eventually retained by the employer and returned to the individual during periods of unemployment) and register as a job seeker at your local *Ufficio di Collocamento*, which is the government employment office responsible for placing workers. (The Italian equivalent of the Job Centre is the Sezione Circoscrizionate per l'Impiego ed il Collocamento in Agricoltura (SCICA). Privately-run employment agencies are not generally allowed to operate in Italy.) In order to be registered in the correct category you will be asked to present copies of your qualifications, either with an official translation or a certificate of equivalence (*certificato di equipollenza* — see Chapter 2). The *Ufficio di Collocamento* will issue you with an *Attestato di Iscrizione* (Registration Card), which must be stamped regularly, and a Certificate of Unemployment. These documents are shown in Figures 15 and 16.

Go to the Ufficio di Collocamento regularly to see jobs that are advertised. Also look for advertisements in newspapers such as *La Repubblica* and *La Stampa* or the Friday job page of *Corriere della Sera*. You could also place an advertisement yourself, Sunday is the best day. The Italian American Heritage Foundation website www.iahfso.org/links.htm has a comprehensive directory of online Italian newspapers.

Other Italian publications worth looking at are the monthly magazines: *Bolletino del Lavoro*, *Campus*, *Trovalavoro* and *Tuttolavoro*. The widely-read, weekly magazine *Mercatone* places advertisements for no cost and has a good section on vacancies. The Career Book, usually on the shelves by October, is issued by the newspaper *Il Sole 24 Ore*, www.careerbooklavoro.somedia.it.

Other institutions you may contact for job vacancies include the Centri Informazione Giovani (Youth Information Centres)

MODULARIO
U.L.M.O. - 63

Mod. C/15

MINISTERO DEL LAVORO E DELLA PREVIDENZA SOCIALE
Ufficio del Lavoro e della Massima Occupazione
di .... ①

Comune di .... ②

Si certifica che il sig. ③ ....

....

è iscritto come disoccupato presso questo Ufficio di Collocamento con la qualifica di ④ ....

al n. ⑤ .... *dal* ⑥ ....

IL DIRIGENTE L'UFFICIO DI COLLOCAMENTO

- Ist. Poligr. e Zecca dello Stato - S.

1. Area unemployment office
2. Municipality
3. Name of unemployed person
4. Qualifications of unemployed person
5. Code number
6. Date on which registered unemployed

Fig. 15. Certificate of unemployment.

Via B. Buozzi, 56
60044 – **FABRIANO (AN)**
Tel. 0732/4306 – Fax 0732/625993
Aut. Min. n. 20/98 del 10/02/98

CURRICULUM VITAE

① ◆ COGNOME _____ ② NOME _____

③ ◆ DATA DI NASCITA _____ ④ LUOGO DI NASCITA _____

⑤ ◆ DOMICILIO _____

⑥ ◆ RESIDENZA _____

⑦ ◆ TELEFONO abitazione _____ ⑧ cellulare _____

⑨ ◆ STATO CIVILE ☐ celibe ☐ nubile ☐ coniugato/a ☐ separato/a ⑩ n° figli _____

⑪ ◆ SERVIZIO MILITARE ☐ assolto ☐ da assolvere ☐ riformato/esonerato

⑫ PATENTE A B C altro : _____ AUTOMUNITO ☐ si ☐ no

⑬ ◆ **TITOLO DI STUDIO** _____

Corsi di Specializzazione

⑭ 1. Titolo _____ Ente Gestore _____ Anno _____

2. Titolo _____ Ente Gestore _____ Anno _____

⑮ ### Conoscenze informatiche

_____

⑯ ### ESPERIENZE DI LAVORO

OCCUPAZIONE ATTUALE _____ Dal _____ presso _____

Qualifica/Mansioni svolte _____

Motivo eventuali dimissioni _____

ULTIMA RETRIBUZIONE Lit. _____

PRECEDENTI ESPERIENZE

• Dal _____ al _____ presso _____

Qualifica/Mansioni svolte _____

Motivo di interruzione del rapporto lavorativo _____

• Dal _____ al _____ presso _____

Qualifica/Mansioni svolte _____

Motivo di interruzione del rapporto lavorativo _____

• Dal _____ al _____ presso _____

Qualifica/Mansioni svolte _____

Motivo di interruzione del rapporto lavorativo _____

Eventuali aziende cui, per motivi di riservatezza, non desidera che il suo Curriculum Vitae sia sottoposto:

1. Surname	9. Married status
2. First name	10. Number of children
3. Date of birth	11. Military service
4. Place of birth	12. Driving licence
5. Domicile	13. Qualification
6. Country of residence	14. Specialised courses
7. Home telephone number	15. IT skills
8. Mobile telephone number	16. Work experience

Fig. 16. Model curriculum vitae.

(see Appendix), Centri di Prima Accogliensa per Stranieri (Reception Centre of Foreigners) or one of the three principal Trades Union head offices which are:

CISL
Via Po 21
00198 Roma
Tel: 06 84731
www.cisl.it

CGIL
Corso d'Italia 25
00198 Roma
Tel: 06 84761

Unione Italiana Del Lavoro
Via Lucullo 6
00187 Roma
Tel: 06 4824005

Places to contact in the UK include:

Overseas Placement Unit
Level 4, Skills House
3–7 Holy Green
Off the Moor
Sheffield S1 4AQ
Tel: 0114 2596051

EURES (European Employment Services) a computerised job information network run by trained Euroadvisers on www.europa.eu or enter your CV into a database for work in the fields of IT, Catering, Healthcare and Air Travel www.eurescv-search.com. (For professional and qualified work only.)

Recruitment and Employment Confederation
36-38 Mortimer Street
London W1N 7RB
Tel: 0800 320588
www.rec.uk.com

More and more employers are searching the Internet for employees and there are many online agencies specialising in the whole of Europe. Two useful sites specialising in Italy are:
www.monsteritalia.it
www.recruitaly.it

After finding a job

When you find a job you can apply for your three-month *Permesso di Soggiorno* (Permit to Stay) to be extended to the regular five-year permit. When doing this remember to take your passport or identity card and a declaration from your employer stating that you are employed. Your employer should then take responsibility for obtaining a work permit by presenting your *Permesso di Soggiorno* to the *Ispettorato del Lavoro* (Labour Inspector) who authorises a work permit. The work permit is then issued by the *Ufficio di Collocamento* (Job Centre).

Opportunities in seasonal work

If you have a job that is not expected to last more than three months you do not need to apply for a *Permesso di Soggiorno*. This also applies to workers who return to their home country at least once a week. However, you should get a statement from your employer declaring the length of your employment.

Most opportunities for short-term employment arise during the summer months. Tourism is one of the main employers, with vacancies becoming available in hotels and restaurants in the tourist resorts. To find a job, first obtain a list of hotels from the tourist office in the region of Italy in which you are interested in working. Then write a letter of application stating your date and place of birth, your work experience, your level of education, your knowledge of foreign languages, your interests, references and a photograph of yourself. Send it off early in the year.

Summer vacancies are also available in holiday villages. However, the conditions usually require someone with training in sports and other skills such as music or drama. The main vacation villages in Italy are organised by the following groups:

Club Mediterranee
Corsia dei Servi 11
Milan
Tel: 02 7735

Touring Club Italiano
Via Adamello 10
Milan
Tel: 02 535991

Valtur
Via Milano 46
Rome
Tel: 06 482100

During harvest time you may be able to find temporary work

on a farm. To find out addresses of farms and agricultural cooperatives where you can apply for work, contact the *Centri Informazione Giovani* (Youth Information Centres) (see Appendix) in the region you are interested in. The main harvests take place as follows, although you should note that there is no great recruitment of foreign workers as in some Mediterranean countries.

- May-August: strawberries, cherries, peaches and plums in Emila Romagna
- September-October: apples and pears in Emilia Romagna, Piedmont and Trentino
- September-October: grapes in Emilia Romagna, Lazio, Piedmont, Puglia, Trentino, Veneto, Tuscany and Marches
- November-December: olives in Puglia, Trentino, Veneto, Tuscany, Marches, Liguria, Calabria and Sicily
- November-December: flowers in Liguria, Tuscany, Lazio and Puglia
- November-December: tobacco in Umbria, Puglia and Campania.

Au pair work

The best way of finding au pair work in Italy is to contact a reputable agency in the UK. The conditions associated with au pairing are clearly stated by the Provincial Labour Office in Italy and stipulate that:

- the worker shall not be under 17 years or over 30 years of age
- the worker shall be guaranteed health and social insurance cover
- the worker shall be given board and lodgings as well as a

sum of money for personal expenses
- working hours must allow at least one day off a week (apart from Sunday) and also time to attend language, cultural or vocational advancement courses.

A person intending to be employed as an au pair must send one of the three copies of the 'Au pair Contract', along with a medical certificate that has been issued within the three previous months, to the local Provincial Labour Office. This office authorises a stay of one year, which is thereafter renewable for another year. This authorisation must then be submitted to the police who will issue a Permit for au pair Employment. Alternatively, ask your host family to accompany you to the provincial police headquarters to inform them that you are a guest and that the purpose of your stay is to learn Italian and not to work.

If all this sounds laborious, it is, and you will probably find that most families simply do not bother, particularly as they are loath to pay the health insurance contributions. If this is the case all well and good, but remember that you will be responsible for your own health insurance. To complicate the scene still further British citizens should note that the UK is not a signatory to the European agreement on au pair placement. In theory this means that British citizens cannot be employed as au pairs in Italy. You will therefore be described as a nanny, mother's help or domestic help, *etc*, in order to avoid the problem. For further information on the conditions of au pair work browse the comprehensive website:

www.aupair.it

English language teaching

There is a big demand in all the major Northern Italian cities for English language teachers. Private language schools tend to have a fast turnover of teachers and so vacancies are regularly available. Vacancies are also to be had within the state education system, although these posts are more difficult to come by and generally less well paid. The system for applying for a teaching job, either in the state or private sectors, is to write a *domanda*, a letter of request. Your letter should include a curriculum vitae and a photograph of yourself, and should state the dates from which you are available for work. If you are already living in Italy you should look out for the **ordinanza**, a decree by which you can enrol yourself onto a teaching register. The *ordinanza* appears in the newspapers and is circulated around schools once every two years. The resulting register, known as the **graduatoria**, is then used by schools in order to fill vacancies. Teachers who are listed on the *graduatoria* have precedence over teachers who make private applications to a school.

Teaching jobs in private language schools tend to be paid by the hour, while state schools pay a salary per month. The state is renowned for the tardy payment of its salaries — be warned! However, a job in a state school is the more secure option as your contract will probably ensure that health and pension contributions are paid on your behalf. If you are employed on a full-time basis, you will be paid the equivalent of 13 months per annum, the month of December being paid double. Contracts with private language schools generally do not involve the payment of health and pension contributions. You will simply have the 19 per cent IRPEF income tax, which is equivalent of PAYE, deducted each month.

Since wages in private language schools are calculated by the hour you should find out whether there are a guaranteed number of working hours, and the policy on being paid for students who book a lesson but do not attend.

Self-employment

The self-employed in Italy are categorised as *indipendente* (independent) and fall under different social security legislation from those that are *dipendente* (dependent). If you are setting up your own business in Italy one of the first things you will want to do is to find a reliable *commercialista* (book-keeper). A *commercialista*, apart from keeping accounts and making tax returns, may also handle the bureaucracy which is involved in starting up a company. The cost of employing a *commercialista*, however, may be something you wish to avoid. In that case, one of the first steps to take in starting up a company (which otherwise the *commercialista* may undertake) is to locate your provincial *Camera di Commercio* (Chamber of Commerce) which will provide information on how to establish your business. You will also need to register at the *Camera di Commercio* (Chamber of Commerce) to obtain a *certificato di iscrizione della Camera di Commercio* (certificate of registration at the Chamber of Commerce). There are also branches of the Italian Chamber of Commerce in the UK (see Appendix of further information for addresses) or go to www.italchamind.org.uk.

Should I register for IVA (VAT)?
At the same time as the procedures above you should make an application to register for **IVA** (VAT). To do this go to the provincial *Ufficio IVA* (VAT Office) and request an application form AA9/5. There is a fixed annual charge to be

registered with IVA as well as other taxes, including the minimum tax that was introduced in 1993 and which all IVA-registered people are obliged to pay. Being IVA-registered also means that you are obliged to pay into the INPS social security and pension scheme. Before rushing ahead and becoming registered make sure that you have enough VAT bills to offset the costs and note that IVA on fuel is only reimbursed to travelling salespersons and representatives. Once you hold the *partita IVA* (VAT registration number) you will be given a *libretto* (booklet) in which to record your bills.

Joining the Professional Register

All private businesses are necessarily classified and registered in an *Albo Professionale* (Professional Register). In order to be entered onto this register you must meet the qualifications required by the Chamber of Commerce. For information about the Chamber of Commerce, website www.camcom.it lists all its activities and addresses nationwide. You may find that you have to sit a routine examination. Some of the main classifications of professional people are given below.

- *libera professionista* (professional man/woman)
- *avvocati* (lawyers)
- *commercialisti* (accountants)
- *medici* (medics)
- *artigiani* (craftsmen)
- *commercianti* (traders)
- *agricolturi* (agriculturists).

Other documentation

If you are establishing a commercial enterprise you must apply for an *Atto Costitutivo della Societa Omologato dal*

Tribunale (memorandum and articles of association ratified by the tribunal). All documents that you obtain during the establishment of your business should be taken to the *Questura* (police headquarters) when you come to renew your *Permesso di Soggiorno.*

MONEY MATTERS

What should be in my contract?

When you sign a work contract, *contratto di lavoro*, check that it indicates the salary and form of payment, the working hours and holidays, the length of the contract and also that it gives a definition of the work and how it should be done. In addition, a contract should state how social security contributions are to be paid. Two-thirds of contributions are normally paid by the employer, the remainder being deducted at source from the employee's salary. A typical contract may state that 24 per cent of your salary is contributed by your employer to the social security fund, while 9 per cent of your earnings is deducted at source. Social security contributions should cover health assistance, sickness benefit and provide an old-age pension. You should also make sure that you are covered by insurance against accidents at work and occupational diseases. The body responsible for this is INAIL, *Istituto Nazionale per l'Assicurazione Contro gli Infortuni sul Lavoro* (National Institution for Insurance Against Accidents at Work). Contracts can only be legally given to people aged 18 or over. However, 16-18 year olds can enter into contracts provided that they are married or are living independently with the consent of a legal guardian.

Income tax

The Italian taxation system, designed to confound the most cunning tax evaders of which Italy has more than its fair share, has, until recently, been fairly unsuccessful. The system is becoming more foolproof now with all information stored on computers, although there are still those who continue to find loopholes, placing ever heavier burdens on the honest tax payer.

The three basic types of income tax are:

- *IRPEF (Imposte sui Reditti delle Persone Fisiche)* which is Personal Income Tax on Italian source income and capital gains

- *IRPEG (Imposte sui Reditti delle Persone Giuridice)* which is Corporate Income Tax, only paid by businesses involved in commerce

- IREP replaced ILOR (both local income taxes) in the 1997 budget.

IRPEF is the tax that affects everybody. It operates in the same way as PAYE in Britain, being regularly deducted. The IRPEF payments are made every month, either by yourself or by your employer at the local tax office. Each time a tax contribution is made be sure to get an official receipt, *attestato di versamento* (see Figure 17). Official receipts are used to settle your final tax bill in your annual *denuncia*, tax return.

On your tax return the amount of IRPEF that is due depends on your salary, calculated on a progressive scale – the higher the income the higher the rate of tax. For an income up to 10,239 Euros the rate is 18 per cent whereas a high income of 69,723 Euros and above is taxed at 44.5 per cent.

Personal allowances to reduce tax liability are:

Basic deduction from 52 Euros to 904 Euros (higher income
= lower allowance)
Allowance for a dependant spouse from 422 Euros to 546
Euros (depending on household income)
Allowance for each child 285 Euros

The individual taxpayer is also entitled to deduct from the gross IRPEF tax selected expenses such as:

Mortgage interest on Italian property
Medical and surgical expenses
Life assurance
University fees in exceptional circumstances

These deductions must be documented and the law provides conditions and limits on the deductibility of these expenses.

If the final outcome of your tax return is that you have paid too much tax then you must request a refund. This is usually done through your local bank by requesting an *accreditamento dei rimborsi IRPEF*. The reimbursement will be paid into your bank account within two to three years.

If you work for an Italian employer you will be taxed at source and you will probably find that your tax return is taken care of. Otherwise it is your responsibility to file a tax return every May or June. The tax return, or *denuncia* as it is known, is difficult to complete even for Italians. You are therefore well advised to employ an *agenzia* (agent), a *consulente di lavoro* (work consultant) or a *commercialista* (accountant). If you are really in trouble you should go to an *Ufficio di Consulenza Fiscale*, a tax consultancy office.

Before approaching a professional make sure you have all relevant documents assembled. These include *buste* (pay-slips), *attestati di versamento* receipts for the payment of any tax you have paid during the year (see facsimile Figure 17), receipts for medical treatment, dental care, donations to charity and any other costs that can be offset against your taxable income. You should also purchase the correct *modulo* (form) on which the tax return is made, either 740 or 101. The *modulo* (form) is sold at *tabacchi* (tobacconists) from the end of April to the end of May.

Indirect taxation

Forms of indirect taxation include:

- IVA (*Imposta sul Valore Aggiunto*, or Value Added Tax) which is the equivalent of UK Value Added Tax and is levied on all goods and services at three rates, 4 per cent, 10 per cent, and the standard rate of 20 per cent. Most foods are taxed at 10 per cent but other consumer items such as clothing, shoes, CD's *etc*, are at the highest rate of 20 per cent.

- ICI (*Imposta Communale sugli Immobili*, or Local Property Tax) is payable yearly, normally in two instalments, on every property by its registered owner, and varies from comune to comune.

- *Imposta di Registro* is a registration tax applicable to transactions and contracts that are subject to IVA. The registration tax is assessed as a percentage.

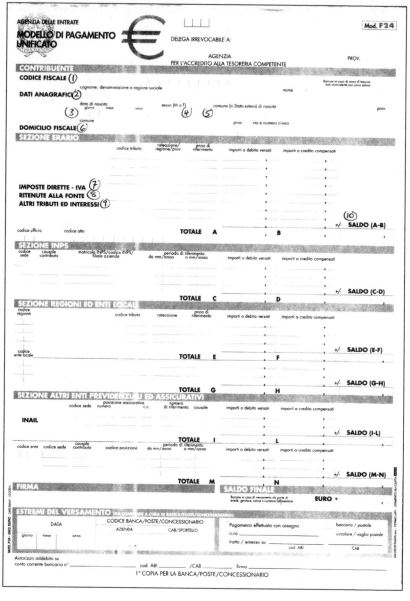

1. Tax code number
2. Surname, name
3. Date of birth (day, month, year)
4. Male/female
5. Place of birth
6. Home address
7. Direct taxation
8. Taxed at source
9. Other contributions and interest
10. Balance

Fig. 17. Standard tax form.

Unemployment benefit

Unemployment benefit in Italy is virtually non-existent. The ordinary allowance, *indennita ordinaria*, is a very meagre sum. It is paid to people who lose their jobs, and who have paid INPS contributions for at least the two preceding years. If you have made contributions in another EU country, these will be taken into account. The allowance is only payable for up to six months.

A special allowance, *trattamenti speciali*, is awarded to dismissed workers in the construction industry and agriculture. The allowance is calculated as a percentage of earnings. In very exceptional cases an extraordinary allowance is granted, the *sussido straordinario*. It is granted to people who are not eligible for the ordinary allowance and who live in specific areas.

To apply for unemployment benefit you must present your notice of dismissal either to your local INPS (National Institute for Social Security) office or to the *Ufficio di Collocamento* (Job Centre), along with a *Stato di Famiglia*, a certificate from your local *Comune* or *Municipio* that indicates the status of your family.

Casual workers, performing artists in the cinema or theatre, workers whose remuneration consists of a share of the profits of an undertaking, and workers whose occupation provides work for less than six months are not normally covered by unemployment insurance. Likewise, those who have never had a job will have great difficulty in claiming unemployment benefit.

The Italian Education System

WHICH SCHOOL ARE YOU GOING TO?

Schools under the Italian State system are free to all dependants of residents of Italy, regardless of nationality, from the age of three until 19. Education is compulsory from age six to 14. All school education, both within the private and public sectors, is controlled by the state and conforms to the curriculum laid down by the *Ministero della Pubblica Istruzione*, MPI (Ministry of Public Education). The management and administration of schools are locally organised, with district school councils and provincial school councils composed of teachers, parents, students and representatives of social and cultural bodies. A certain amount of local autonomy is also permitted within the structure of experimental courses that are held at secondary level. Vocational education, outside technical secondary schools (under the MPI), is mainly the responsibility of individual regions. Generally speaking you will find that education is at a considerably higher standard in the North of Italy than in the South.

The school year runs from mid-September to mid-June. Classes are generally held in the mornings only, but six mornings a week. From primary level upwards, students are expected to spend their afternoons doing homework and private study.

Low-achieving children and those with minor handicaps are integrated in normal classes, but usually have a special teacher who dedicates extra time within the class.

Pre-primary

The state provides at least one *Scuola Materna* (Nursery School) in every Italian town for children aged from three to six years old. Children attending pre-school are organised into groups with a minimum of 15 and a maximum of 25. If a handicapped pupil is integrated in the class the maximum is 20. As it is not obligatory, it is generally attended by children with working parents. The doors open at 8 am and usually close at 5.30 pm with lunch and transport provided at a daily charge. Waiting lists for nursery schools can be for two or three years so make sure you register in plenty of time. There are also numerous private nursery schools, some of which are run by Catholic organisations. Around Rome and the cities of Northern Italy you will find a number of private nursery schools that are conducted in English. However, you can expect to pay considerable fees.

Primary school

Scuola Elementare (Elementary School) covers five years from the age of six to 11. It is divided into a two year lower cycle and a three year upper cycle. The school day is four hours long, during which time children are under continual assessment of both their personality and behaviour as well as their educational achievements, all of which is recorded on *schede* (personal cards). If the required achievements are not reached pupils do not graduate from one year to the next, but repeat the year. On completion of the elementary school an examination is set in order to graduate to middle school.

Lower secondary school

Scuola Media (middle school) education is compulsory for three years, for children from the age of 11 to 14. It is the only possible way of completing compulsory education. The school day is of five or six hours duration. Assessment is based on an annual evaluation by the class teacher who writes a report on the student's behaviour, attitudes, tendencies and level of achievement. At the end of the three years an examination is taken in order to graduate to upper secondary school with a *Licenza Elementare* (Primary School Diploma).

Upper secondary school

Scuola Secondaria di II Grado (upper secondary school) is obligatory until a student's 17th birthday. Students may then leave school or continue for another three years at the end of which they may go onto higher education or enter the job market. There are five basic types of secondary school:

- Liceo Classico (Classics Lyceum)
- Liceo Scientifico (Scientific Lyceum)
- Liceo Artistico (Artistic Lyceum)
- Istituto Tecnico (Technical Institute)
- Istituto Professionale (Vocational Institute).

The Classics, Artistic and Scientific schools tend to be attended by students who intend to go on to university. The Technical and Vocational Institutes tend to lead directly to specific careers. Upper secondary education is completed by taking a level of *maturita*. The final marks, on a scale of

0–60, have 36 as the minimum pass grade. For school work marking is on a scale of 0–10 with six as the pass mark. *Maturita* is roughly the equivalent of A levels.

English-speaking schools

International schools and other private schools hold tuition in English, and are run by British and American teachers and administrators. Below is a list of the principal English-speaking schools in Italy, and there is an extensive listing on www.ecis.org – the website of:

The European Council of International Schools,
21B Lavant Street
Petersfield
Hants
GU32 3EL

Rome International School
Viale Romania 32
00197 Roma
Tel: 06 84482650.
(age range 3–14 years)

American Overseas School of Rome
Via Cassia 811
00189 Roma
Tel: 06 334381
(age range 3-20 years)

Marymount International School
Via di Villa Lauchli 180
00191 Roma

Tel: 06 36301742
(age range 3-18 years)

St George's English School
Via Cassia – La Storta
00123 Roma
Tel: 06 3086001
(age range 3-18 years)

St Stephen's School
Via Aventina 3
00153 Roma
Tel: 06 5750605
(age range 14-19)

St James Henderson British School Milan
Via Pisano Dossi 16
20134 Milano
Tel: 02 26413332
(age range 3-18)

The International School of Milan
Monza Section
Via Ramazzotti 28A
20052 Milano
Tel: 039 2496015
(age range 3-19)

American School of Milan
20090 Novaresco di Opera
Milano
Tel: 02 5300001
(age range 3-19)

Americana International School Genoa
Via Quarto 13
16148 Genoa
Tel: 010 386528
(age range 3-14)

English International School of Padua
Via Forcellini 168
35128 Padua
Tel: 049 8022503
(age range 3-14)

The International School of Naples
Building A
HQ AFSOUTH Post
Viale della Liberazione 1
Bagnoli
Napoli
Tel: 081 7212037
(age range 3-18)

American International School of Florence
Via del Carota 23/25
Bagno a Ripoli
50012 Firenze
Tel: 055 6461007

International School of Trieste
Via Conconello 16, Opicina
34016 Trieste
Tel: 040 211452

FURTHER EDUCATION

University

The universities of Rome, Naples, Milan, Bologna and Turin account for half the university population of Italy. There are, however, 65 universities in total, all of which are run by the State. This includes four officially recognised private universities, three polytechnics, three special institutions of higher education, eight university institutes of education and 21 higher institutes of physical education. There are also two schools of Italian language and culture, namely the Universita Italiana per Stranieri di Perugia and the Scuola di Lingua e Cultura Italiana per Stranieri di Siena. Many of Italy's universities date back centuries: Bologna University is the oldest in Europe, founded in 1088.

A foreign student in Italy can take university courses at the following levels, provided they have the necessary admission requirements and pass the Italian language course exam. The official tuition is in Italian and the exam is usually held in the first half of September, prior to the beginning of the next academic year. Foreign students holding the certificates issued by the Universita per Stranieri di Perugia and the Universita per Stranieri di Siena may be exempted from the language exam.

- *Diplomi Universitari (DU)*
- *Diploma di Laurea (DL)*
- *Diploma di Specialista (DS)*
- *Dottorato di Ricerca (DR)*

The Diplomi Universitari involves two- to three-year courses leading to a diploma. The *Corsi di Laurea*, which are for four or five years, or in the case of medicine six years, are courses leading to the *Laurea* diploma and the title *Dottore* (doctor). *Post Lauream*, specialised courses and research doctorates last a minimum of two and three years respectively.

The university system is organised so that anybody who has attended secondary school and has a Diploma di Maturita (or comparable foreign qualification) has the right to go to university. There are no interviews and no qualification specifications (apart from secondary school diploma). As a result the popular courses are excessively overcrowded, but due to the rigour and expense of university education drop-out numbers are amongst the highest in Europe. Twenty-five per cent of students enrolled in the 1995/6 academic year abandoned their course of study between the first and second years. In recent years there has been a growing tendency to introduce entrance tests.

The negative aspects of university in Italy include the high cost of accommodation and the limited availability of halls of residence, or any other subsidised student housing. For this reason, most Italian students go to the university in their home town or as close by as possible so that they can continue living at home. The accommodation problem is exacerbated when students fail to pass their annual examinations and so have to repeat the year. The average age of a graduate is 27 years. The good news is that there are no tuition fees as such, instead there are annual taxes that are paid on registration. It is necessary to complete the registration procedure every year when taxes are updated. The tax varies from faculty to faculty; first year enrolments range from 3,612 Euros to 8,012 Euros.

Information for foreigners wishing to attend Italian university can be obtained by writing to the relevant university and requesting the *Guida per lo Studente Straniero* (Guide for the Foreign Student) Alternatively browse the informative website www.transworldeducation.com.

Study grants

Grants are awarded to Italian students whose family's income falls within a certain bracket. If you are an EU citizen with family resident in Italy you have the same rights as Italian nationals to apply for a university grant. The first step in applying for a grant is to contact the *Ente per il Diritto allo Studio Universitario* at the university or education institute of your choice. Grants are not administered on a national level and so the amount of benefit you receive varies from place to place.

If you are a foreign student whose parents are not resident in Italy you are unlikely to be awarded an Italian grant but you may apply for financial aid from an international body. One way of finding out information about grant-giving bodies is to consult the Noopolis Databank, a non-profit making organisation that continuously updates its data on grants and scholarships. The databank can be consulted at all Italian universities as well as some student welfare offices and youth information offices (see Appendix). For further information on the databank write with your personal details to the Noopolis head office:

Noopolis
Centro Internazionale Sviluppo e Cooperazione Culturale
Via Domenico Tardini 35

00167 Roma
Tel: 06 6633103
www.noopolis.com

An annual sum of money is also allocated to foreign students wishing to attend Italian university, by the Italian Ministry of Foreign Affairs. For further information contact the Ministry at the address below, or consult an Italian Cultural Institute abroad (see Appendix for addresses).

Ministero Affari Esteri Centralino
Piazzale Farnesina 1
00194 Roma
Tel: 06 36911

The Erasmus Programme, which is funded by the European Commission, is another organisation you might wish to apply to for financial support. It offers scholarships and loans to university students who wish to complete a part of their studies in Italy (or any other EU country). For further information on Erasmus contact:

Erasmus Bureau
Rue Montoyer 70
B-1040 Brussels
Tel: 02 2330111

The national agency for the administration of Erasmus scholarships in Italy is as follows:

Direzione Istruzione Universitaria
Erasmus

Ministero della Pubblica Istruzione
Viale Trastevere 76
Roma
Tel: 06 58491

The national agency in Britain for Erasmus is:

UK Socrates-Erasmus Council
R+D Building
The University
Canterbury
Kent CT2 7PD
Tel: 01227 762712

www.erasmus.ac.uk

Otherwise you may wish to support yourself by taking up a part-time job. Note, however, that as a student at an Italian university it is against the law to work for more than 500 hours per year.

Applying for Italian university

Foreign students wishing to attend an Italian university should apply through the Italian Consulate in their home country in January. The Consulate will send a list of the required documents, which includes an E111, and an application form on which you are to select four universities, placing them in order of preference. On receipt of the application the Consulate will send EU citizens an identity card that is stamped with a consul's visa, while non-EU citizens are issued with a student visa. These documents are to be presented to the *Questura* (Police Headquarters) within eight days of arriving in Italy, in order to receive a *Permesso di Soggiorno* (Permit to Stay).

Foreign students whose parents, sisters, brothers or spouse are resident in Italy should apply by addressing themselves in person to the university of their choice. You will be asked to submit a formal application bearing the correct denomination of *bolli* (state stamps). In addition you should enclose your original educational certificates, birth certificate, recent photographs and receipt of payment of registration tax.

Foreign students are also expected to sit an Italian language examination before being admitted. If the exam is failed then foreign students who have applied for university from overseas are obliged to return to their home country.

ITALIAN COURSES FOR FOREIGNERS

Italian language and culture courses

There are a good number of Italian language and culture courses for foreign students held in Italian universities as well as at private schools. The courses generally range from two to 12 weeks' duration, with food and accommodation available at an additional cost. Language courses are held at all levels and the courses on Italian culture cover a wide spectrum of subjects ranging from Etruscan History to Contemporary Italian Literature. Florence has the greatest concentration of courses on offer with around 25 private language schools in operation. Perhaps the widest ranging courses are offered by the Universita Italiana per Stranieri, in Perugia, and the Scuola di Lingua e Cultura per Stranieri in Siena, both of which are funded by the State. It is possible to apply for grants to attend either of these schools. The grants are funded by the schools themselves and also by the Ministero degli Affari Esteri (Italian Ministry for Foreign Affairs). To find out more about grants apply to your local Italian Consulate or Italian Cultural Institute (see Appendix for addresses).

Attending an Italian course at either of the above schools or in a university is generally less expensive than enrolling at a private school. The disadvantage of language courses at universities is that they are often only held during the summer, and not all year round, as they are in private schools or at the state schools in Perugia and Siena.

The addresses for the schools in Perugia and Siena are given below, as are the addresses of Italian universities that hold Italian language courses. Request the annual programme for further information and the cost of registration fees and accommodation.

Universita Italiana per Stranieri (USP)
Palazzo Gallenga
Piazza Fortebraccio 4
06123 Perugia
Tel: 075 5746218

Universita per Stranieri di Siena
Via Pantaneto
4553100 Siena
Tel: 0577 240111

Centro Linguistico Italiano Dante Alighieri

Piazza Della Republica 5
50125 Firenze
Tel: 055 210808

Accademia del Giglio
Via Ghibellina 116
50122 Firenze
Tel: 055 2302467

Centro Internazionale di Studi Italiani
Universita degli Studi di Genova
Via Balbi 5
16126 Genoa
Tel: 010 20991
www.unige.it

Corsi Internazionali di Lingua e Cultura Italiana
Universita degli Studi di Milano
Via Comelico 39–41
20135 Milano
Tel: 02 55006 324

Centro Linguistico di Ateneo
Universita degli Studi di Parma
Via Universitá 12
43100 Parma
Tel: 0521 032111
www.unipr.it

Centro Interfacolta per L'Apprendimento delle Lingue
Universita degli Studi di Trento
Via Bomporto Bernadino 2
38100 Trento
Tel: 0461 881111

Universita degli Studi di Urbino
Via Saffi 2
61029 Urbino
Tel: 0722 3051

Centro Linguistico Interfacolta
Universita degli Studi di Venezia
Castello
30122 Venice
Tel: 041 5203055

Other courses for foreigners

There is a selection of private courses designed for foreign students, ranging from art restoration to tourism and marketing. The courses last from two weeks to one year. Contact the following addresses for further information.

The British Institute of Florence
Piazza Strozz 2
Lungarno Guicciardini
50123 Firenze
Tel: 055 284033

Istituto per l'Arte e il Restauro
Palazzo Spinelli
Borgo Santa Croce 10
50122 Firenze
Tel: 055 240172
(art, fashion, language)

Istituto Per L'arte E il Restauro
Via Maggio 13

50125 Firenze
Tel: 055 282951
(graphics and interior design)

Scuola di Oreficeria
Via Maggio 13
50125 Firenze
Tel: 055 282951
(jewellery)

Europass SNC Scuola per Stranieri
Via Sant Egidio 12
50122 Firenze
Tel: 055 2345802

Centro Pontevecchio Didattican E Consulenza Linguistica
Piazza della Signoria 4A
50122 Firenze
Tel: 055 294511
(cookery, gardening, language, painting)

Istituto Italiano Arte Artigianato e Restauro
Viale di Porta Ardeatina 108
00154 Roma
Tel: 06 5757185
(crafts and restoration)

Istituto Venezia
Dorsoduro 3116A
Venezia 30123
Tel: 041 5224331
www.istitutovenezia.com

THE CASE OF THE ITALIAN STUDENT

Carla, an Italian student, after five years of studying political science was told that she would have to sit an English examination. She received no preparation for it on her course and when she took it, failed. But there again so did all 118 other students on her course. Two passed! Carla took private English lessons for six months, only to fail again as the examination format had been changed without her being informed. After six more months of private lessons she was ready to take it again but had to hang around the university for over a week as no date had been announced and it could be any minute. Finally she did take the exam, and passed, and so completed her degree.

Advice: never give up but avoid the higher education system if at all possible! It isn't run for the benefit of the students!

Appendix of Further Information

USEFUL ADDRESSES ABROAD AND UK

Italian Cultural Institutes

Italian Cultural Institute
39 Belgrave Square
London SW1X 8NT
UK
Tel: 020 7235 1461
www.italcultur.org.uk

Italian Cultural Institute
82 Nicholson Street
Edinburgh EH8 9EW
UK
Tel: 0131 668 2777
www.italcult.net/edimburgo

British Italian Society
21/22 Grosvenor Street
London W1X 9FE
UK
Tel: 020 7495 5536
www.british-italian.org

Italian Cultural Institute
11 Fitzwilliam Square
Dublin 2
Eire
Tel: (00353-1) 6766662
www.iol.ie/-italcult

Italian Cultural Institute
2025 M Street, NW
Suite 610
Washington DC 20036
USA
Tel: (001-202) 2239800
www.italcultusa.org

Italian Cultural Institute
686 Park Avenue
New York NY 10021
USA
Tel: (001-212) 8794242
www.italcultny.org

Italian Cultural Institute
500 North Michigan Avenue
Suite 1450
Chicago IL 60611
USA
Tel: (001-312) 8229545
www.iicch.org

Italian Cultural Institute
425 Washington Street
Suite 200
San Francisco
CA 94111
USA
Tel: (001-415) 788 7142
www.sfiic.org

Italian Cultural Institute
1023 Hilgard Avenue
Los Angeles
CA 90024
USA
Tel: (001-310) 443 3250
www.iicusa.org

Italian Cultural Institute
1200 Penfield Ave
Montreal
Quebec H3A 1A9
Canada
Tel: (001-514) 8493473
www.italcultur-qc.org

Italian Cultural Institute
496 Huron Street
Toronto
Ontario M5R 2R3
Canada
Tel: (001-416) 9622503
www.iicto-ca.org

Italian Cultural Institute

510 West Hastings St
Suite 500
Vancouver
BC V6B IL8
Canada
Tel: (001-604) 6880809
www.cvan-ca.org

Italian Consulates and Embassies

Italian Consulate General
38 Eaton Place
London SW1X 8AN
UK
Tel: 020 7235 9371
www.embitaly.org.uk

Italian Embassy
14 Three Kings Yard
London W1K 4EH
UK
Tel: 020 7312 2200
www.embitaly.org.uk

Italian Consulate
32 Melville Street
Edinburgh EH3 7HA
UK
Tel: 0131 226 3631

Italian Consulate
111 Piccadilly
Manchester M1 2HY
UK
Tel: 0161 236 9024

Italian Vice-Consulate
    7–9 Greyfriars
    Bedford MK40 1HJ
    UK
    Tel: 01234 356647

Italian Embassy
    63 Northumberland Road
    Dublin 4
    Eire
    Tel: (00353-1) 6601744

Italian Embassy
    275 Slater Street
    21st Floor
    Ottawa
    Ontario
    KIP 5H9
    Canada
    Tel: (001-613) 2322401
    www.italincanada.com

Italian Embassy
    3000 Whitehaven Street NW
    Washington DC 20008
    USA
    Tel: (001-202) 6124400
    www.italyemb.org

Italian State Tourism Offices

Italian State Tourist Office
    1 Princes Street
    London W1R 8AY
    UK

Tel: 020 7355 1439
www.enit.it

Italian State Tourism Office
    175 Bloor Street East
    Suite 907
    South Tower
    Toronto
    Ontario M4W 3R8
    Canada
    Tel: 00416 925 4882

Italian State Tourist Office
    630 Fifth Avenue
    Suite 1565
    New York
    NY10111
    USA
    Tel: 001-212 586-9249

Italian Trade Institutes

Italian Trade Centre (ICE)
    37 Sackville Street
    London W1X 2DQ
    UK
    Tel: 020 7734 2412

Italian Chamber of Commerce
    1 Prince's Street
    London W1B 2AY
    UK
    Tel: 020 7495 8191

Italian Chamber of Commerce
    52 Ardwick Green South

Manchester MI39 9XF
Tel: 0161 2744168

Italian Institute for Foreign Trade
16 St Stephen's Green
Dublin 2
Eire
Tel: 03531 6767829

Other useful addresses

DEFRA
1A Page Street
London SW1 P4PQ
Tel: 0207 9046000

Automobile Association
Fanum House
PO Box 51
Basingstoke
Hants RG21 4EA
UK
Tel: 01256 469777 or
0870 6000375
www.theAA.com

Banca d'Italia
39 King Street
London EC2V 8JJ
UK
Tel: 020 7606 4201

Benefits Agency
Pensions & Overseas Benefit
Directorate

Benton
Newcastle upon Tyne
NE98 1BA
UK
Tel: 0191 218 2000

British Council of Scotland
The Tun, 4 Jackson's Entry
Holyrood Road
Edinburgh EH8 8PJ
UK
Tel: 0131 5245700
www.britishcouncil.org/
scotland

Contributions Agency
Department of Social Security
Overseas Branch
Tyneview Park
Whiteley Road
Newcastle upon Tyne
NE98 1BA
UK
Tel: 0191 218 7777

Department of Trade and
Industry
1 Victoria Street
London SW1H 0ET
UK
Tel: 020 7215 5000
www.dti.gov.uk

Royal Automobile Club
PO Box 100

RAC House
Lansdowne Road
Croydon CR9 2JA
UK
www.rac.co.uk

Royal Scottish Automobile
Club
   11 Blythswood Square
   Glasgow G2 4AG
   UK
   Tel: 0141 221 3850
   www.rsac.co.uk

USEFUL ADDRESSES IN ITALY

Foreign Consulates and Embassies

British Embassy
   Porta Pia
   Via XX Settembre 80a
   00187 Roma
   Tel: 06 42200001

British Consulate
   PO Box 679
   Dorsoduro 1051
   30123 Venezia
   Tel: 041 5227207/5227408

British Consulate
   Viale Colombo 160

09045 Cagliari
Tel: 070 828628

British Consulate
   Palazzo Castelbarco
   Lungarno Corsini 2
   Florence 50123
   Tel: 055 284133

British Consulate
   Via di Francia 28
   16149 Genoa
   Tel: 010 416828

British Consulate
   Via San Paolo 7
   20121 Milano
   Tel: 02 723001

British Consulate
   Via dei Mille 40
   80121 Napoli
   Tel: 081 4238911

British Consulate
   Via Dante Alighieri
   34122 Trieste
   Tel: 040 3478303

Canadian Consulate General
   Via Vittor Pisani 19
   20124 Milano
   Tel: 02 67581

Canadian Embassy
Via G. B. de Rossi 27
00161 Roma
Tel: 06 445981

Irish Embassy
Piazza di Campitelli 3
00186 Roma
Tel: 06 6979121

USA Embassy
Via Vittorio Veneto 119/A
00187 Roma
Tel: 06 46741

British Council
Via IV Fontane 20
00184 Roma
Tel: 06 478141

British Chamber of Commerce
for Italy
Via Dante 12
20121 Milano
Tel: 02 876981

Ministries

Ministero della Pubblica
Istruzione
(Ministry of Public
Education)
Viale Trastevere 76/A
00194 Roma
Tel: 06 58491

Ministero degli Affari Esteri
(Ministry of Foreign Affairs)
Ufficio IX
Piazzale Farnesina 1
00194 Roma
Tel: 06 36911

Youth Information Centres

Informagiovani
Via Alfieri Vittorio 2
15100 Alessandria
Tel: 0131 266079

Informagiovani
Via Marco Polo 53
Quartiere Navile
40131 Bologna
Tel: 051 6345550

Sportello Comunale
Informagiovani
Palazzo Coppa
Piazza Gramsci Antonio
81100 Caserta
Tel: 0823 355561

Servizio Informagiovani
Vicolo Santa Maria
Maggiore 1
50123 Firenze
Tel: 055 218310

Informagiovani
Via Goldoni 83

57125 Livorno
Tel: 0586 899123

Informagiovani
Via Marconi 1
20123 Milano
Tel: 02 62085215

Centro Informazioni
Documentazione Giovani
Corso Cavallotti Felice 21
28100 Novara
Tel: 0321 623270

Informagiovani
Vicolo Ponte Molino 7
35137 Padova
Tel: 049 654328

Centro Informagiovani
Via Guido Da Polenta 4
48100 Ravenna
Tel: 05 4436494

Informagiovani
Via Captain Bavastro 94
00154 Roma
Tel: 06 5756759

Centro Informazione
Documentazione Giovani
Via delle Orfane 20
10122 Torino
Tel: 011 4424977
www.commune.torino.it

Centro Informagiovani
Corso Portoni Borsari 17
37121 Verona
Tel: 045 8010795

Other useful addresses

INPS
Via Ciro il Grande 21
00144 Roma
Tel: 06 59051

Automobile Club Italiano
Via Marsala 8
00185 Roma
Tel: 06 491115
www.aci.it

USEFUL WEBSITES

www.paginegialle.it
Italian yellow pages telephone directory
www.paginebianche.it
Italian telephone directory
www.britain.it
British Embassy in Rome
www.embitaly
Italian embassy in London
www.esteri.it
Italian Ministry of Foreign
Affairs
www.noiitaliani.com
Italian Consulate London
www.italculture.org.uk

Italian Cultural Institute London
www.enit.it
Italian State Tourist Board
www.payaway.co.uk/italy
Job finder – working holidays, gap year
www.inlandrevenue.gov
Information on living and working abroad
www.theaa.com
Automobile Association
www.aci.it
Automobile Club d'Italia
www.lifeinitaly.com
Renting and buying property in Italy
www.informer.it
General advice for living in Italy
www.noopolis.com
Scholarship database
www.erasmus.ac.uk
Socrates/Erasmus university exchange
www.comunetorino.it
Youth information
www.romebuddy.com
Travel advice for Rome
www.navigazionelaqhi.it
Crossing Italian lakes
www.hostetler.net/italy
Italian national holidays

ABBREVIATIONS OF PROVINCES

The following is an alphabetical list of the abbreviations that are used for each of Italy's 95 provinces. You will see the abbreviations appear in post codes and in official documents.

AG	Agrigento
AL	Alessandria
AN	Ancona
AO	Aosta
AP	Ascoli Piceno
AQ	Aquila
AR	Arezzo
AT	Asti
AV	Avellino
BA	Bari
BG	Bergamo
BL	Belluno
BN	Benevento
BO	Bologna
BR	Brindisi
BS	Brescia
BZ	Bolzano
CA	Cagliari
CB	Campobasso
CE	Caserta
CH	Chieti
CL	Caltanisetta
CN	Cuneo
CO	Como
CR	Cremona

CS	Cosenza	PR	Parma
CT	Catania	PS	Pesaro
CZ	Catanzaro	PT	Pistoia
EN	Enna	PV	PaVia
FE	Ferrara	PZ	Potenza
FG	Foggia	RA	Ravenna
FI	Firenze	RC	Reggio Calabria
FO	Forli	RE	Reggio Emilia
FR	Frosinone	RG	Ragusa
GE	Genova	RI	Rieti
GO	Gorizia	RO	Rovigo
GR	Grosseto	ROMA	Roma
IM	Imperia	SA	Salerno
IS	Isernia	SI	Siena
LE	Lecce	SO	Sondrio
LI	Livorno	SP	Spezia
LT	Latina	SR	Siracusa
LU	Lucca	SS	Sassari
MC	Macerata	SV	Savona
ME	Messina	TA	Taranto
MI	Milano	TE	Teramo
MN	Mantova	TN	Trento
MO	Modena	TO	Torino
MS	Massa Carrara	TP	Trapani
MT	Matera	TR	Terni
NA	Napoli	TS	Trieste
NO	Novara	TV	Treviso
NU	Nuoro	UD	Udine
OR	Oristano	VA	Varese
PA	Palermo	VC	Vercelli
PC	Piacenza	VE	Venezia
PD	Padova	VI	Vicenza
PE	Pescara	VR	Verona
PG	Perugia	VT	Viterbo
PI	Pisa		
PN	Pordenone		

ALPHABET BY NAMES

The following alphabetical list is used by all Italians to spell out words, especially over the telephone.

A	Ancona
B	Bologna
C	Como
D	Domodossola
E	Empoli
F	Firenze
G	Genova
H	Hotel
I	Imola
K	Kursaal
L	Livorno
M	Milano
N	Napoli
O	Otranto
P	Padova
Q	Quarto
R	Roma
S	Savona
T	Torino
U	Udine
V	Venezia
W	Washington
X	Ics
Y	York or Yacht
Z	Zara

SOME FAMOUS ITALIANS TO KNOW

National leaders

Giuseppe Mazzini (1805-1872). The father of unified Italy.

Giuseppe Garibaldi (1808-1882). National hero and protagonist in unification of Italy.

Benito Mussolini (1883-1945). Fascist leader and founder of fascist party in 1921.

Medici, Cosimo the Elder (1389-1464). First Medici ruler.

Medici, Lorenzo the Magnificent (1449-1492). Medici ruler known for his patronage of the arts.

Camillo de Cavour (1810-1861). Diplomat central to the unification of Italy.

Writers, playwrights, poets

Luigi Pirandello (1867-1936). Writer and playwright of *Six Characters in Search of an Author.*

Alighieri Dante (1265-1321). Florentine poet, widely known for the *Divine Comedy.*

Francesco Petrarch (1304-1374). Poet who has lent his name to literary term 'petrarchism'.

Giovanni Boccaccio (1313-1375). Writer whose best known works include *The Decameron.*

Niccolo Macchiavelli (1469-1527). Wrote *The Prince*, known as the handbook for despots.

Benvenuto Cellini (1500-1571). Writer, provided a vivid record of 16th century life.

Alberto Moravia (born 1907). Pseudonym of the writer Alberto Pincherle.

Primo Levi (1919-1987). Writer who wrote of his experience of a Nazi war camp.

Gabriele d'Annunzio (1863-1938). Poet known for his decadent lifestyle and bizarre poetry.

Carlo Levi (1902-1975). Writer and painter, author of *Christ Stopped at Eboli.*

Painters, sculptors

Sandro Botticelli (1444-1510). Influential 15th century Florentine painter.

Buonarroti Michelangelo (1475-1564). Painted, among many outstanding works, the Sistine Chapel.

Leonardo da Vinci (1452-1519). Known as the Renaissance Universal Man.

Sanzio Rafaello (Raphael) (1483-1520). One of the great creators of the Renaissance.

Vecellio Tiziano (Titian) (1487/90-1576). Important Venetian painter.

Gianlorenzo Bernini (1598-1680). Tuscan sculptor.

Giorgio Vasari (1511-1574). Primarily an art historian although also painted and practised architecture.

Duccio di Buoninsegna (1255/60-1315/18). Master Sienese painter.

Donatello (c1386-1466). Greatest sculptor in Florence before Michelangelo.

Giovanni Cimabue (c1240-1302). Artist often associated with Giotto.

Fra Angelico (1387-1455). Painter and Domenican friar.

Piero della Francesca (1410-1492). One of best-loved painters of 15th century.

Jacopo Tintoretto (1518-1594). Venetian Mannerist painter.

Andrea Palladio (1508-1580). Influential Italian architect.

Paolo Veronese (1528-1588). Verona artist, influenced by Titian.

Antonio Canaletto (1697-1768). Famous for paintings of Venice views.

Amedeo Modigliani (1884-1920). Greatest Italian painter of 20th century.

Giorgio Dechirico (1888-1978). Quasi surrealist painter.

Michelangelo Merisi Caravaggio (1573-1610). Painter of realist style.

Andrea Mantegna (1410-1506). Painter, influenced by Donatello.

Antonio Correggio (1489-1534). Worked as a painter in Parma; his style anticipated the Baroque.

Scientists

Galilei Galileo (1564-1642). Scientist and mathematician who evolved theories on gravity and the pendulum.

Guglielmo Marconi (1874-1937). Invented the first radio.

Luigi Galvani (1737-1798). Anatomist, discovered electricity in animals.

Enrico Fermi (1901- 1954). Made first sustained nuclear reaction.

Alessandro Volta (1747-1827). Physicist, discovered the electrical volt.

Evangelista Torricelli (1608-1647). Mathematician and physicist; invented the mercury barometer.

Religious figures

St Francis of Assisi (1181-1226). Founder of the Franciscan Order.

St Anthony of Padua (1195-1231). Born in Portugal but preached and died in Padua.

St Benedict (c480-547). Father of western monasticism.

St Bernardine of Siena (1380-1444). Influential leader in Franciscan movement.

St Bona of Pisa (1156-1207). Patron saint of travellers.

St Callistus the First (died 222). Pope and martyr.

St Catherine of Siena (c1347-1380). Now considered a doctor of the church.

St Celestine the First (died 432). Bishop of Rome in 422.

St Celestine the Fifth (1214-1296). Eighty year old hermit elected pope, died after ten months.

St Charles Borromeo (1538-1584). Bishop and cardinal, of aristocratic descent.

St Clare of Assisi (1194-1253). Founded order of Poor Clares in association with St Francis.

St Clement the First (died end of 1st century). First of apostolic fathers, symbol is the anchor.

St Francis Borgia (1510-1572). Jesuit and great grandson of ill-reputed Pope Alexander VI.

St Ambrose (334-397). One of the great Latin doctors of the church.

St Gregory the Great (540-604). First and greatest of 16 popes of same name.

St Gregory the Seventh (1020-1085). Heralded an era of ecclesiastical reform.

St Januarius (died 305?). A phial of this saint's blood is kept in the cathedral at Naples and is said to liquefy at auspicious moments.

St Lawrence (died 258). Martyred by being grilled on a grid.

St Leo the Great (died 461). Bishop of Rome, influential in early history of papacy.

St Martin the First (died 655). Pope and martyr.

St Paul of the Cross (1694-1775). Founded order of Passionists devoted to Saviour's cross and Passion.

St Peter Orseolo (928-987). Doge of Venice.

St Pius the Fifth (1504-1572). Pope and friar of the Domenican order.

St Pius the Tenth (1835-1914). Pope while state and church were separated in France.

St Scholastica (c480-543). Sister of St Benedict.

St Silvester the First (died 335). Pope and first non-martyr to be made a saint.

St Thomas Aquinas (1225-1274). Theologian and doctor of the church.

St Valentine (date unknown). Feast day 14th February.

Musicians

Antonio Vivaldi (1676-1741). Composer and musician; among his best known works is the *Four Seasons*.

Vincenzo Bellini (1801-1856). Composer of opera.

Gaetano Donizetti (1797-1848). Composed more than 60 operas.

Gioacchino Rossini (1792-1868). Composed many operas including the *Barber of Seville.*

Giuseppe Verdi (1813-1901). Composer of operas including *Rigoletto, La Traviata, Aida.*

Nicolo Paganini (1782-1840). Violinist and composer.

Alessandro Scarlatti (1660-1725). Composed Neopolitan operas popular in 18th century.

Giacomo Puccini (1858-1924). Composed operas including *La Bohème, Tosca, Madame Butterfly.*

Claudio Monteverdi (1567-1924). Composed some of earliest major operatic works.

Luciano Pavarotti (born 1936). Tenor, eminent in the world of opera.

Arturo Toscanini (1867-1957). Conductor of concerts and operas.

Antonio Stradivari (1645-1737). One of family of violin makers in Cremona.

Film-makers

Luchino Visconti (1906-1976). Neo-realist film-maker.

Roberto Rossellini (1906-1977). Made many films starring Ingrid Bergman.

Federico Fellini (1920-). Amalgamated neo-realist ideals.

Michelangelo Antonioni (1912-). Neo-realist film-maker.

Francesco Rosi (1922-) Often worked with Visconti.

Pier Paolo Pasolini (1922-1975). Film-maker and writer.

Franco Zeffirelli (1923-). Amongst most recent films was *Who's Afraid of Virginia Woolf.*

Explorers

Marco Polo (1254-1324). Travelled across Asia to Peking.

Cristoforo Colombo (1447-1506). Credited with the discovery of America.

Education

Maria Montessori (1870-1952). Created the Montessori method of education.

Glossary

PASSPORTS, VISAS AND PERMITS

certificato di equipollenza	certificate of academic equivalence
certificato residenza	residence permit
cittadino	nationality
codice fiscale	fiscal code number
domicilio	address
firma	signature
giorno	day
nome, cognome	forename, surname
passaporto	passport
permesso di soggiorno	permit to stay
scopo lavorativo	for the purpose of work
scopo residenza	for the purpose of residence
sottoscritto	undersigned
Ufficio Anagrafe	Municipal Registry Office
Ufficio Collocamento	Italian Employment Office
Ufficio Imposte Dirette	Provincial Tax Office
Ufficio Stranieri	Foreign Department
valido (fino al)	valid (until)

TRAVEL

abbonamento	season ticket
Automobile Club d'Italia (ACI)	Italian Automobile Club
autostrada	motorway
benzina normale/super	regular/super grade petrol
biglietto, biglietti, biglietteria	ticket, tickets/ticket office

Carta Verde	Youth Rail Card
chilometrico	ticket allowing 3,000km free rail travel
conducento anonimo	unnamed driver
corso	main street, boulevard
entrata	entrance
Ferrovie Statale	State Railway System
mezza pensione	half board
Ministero del Trasporto	Ministry of Transport
numero targa	number plate
incrocio	crossroads
lavori in corso	road works ahead
passaggio a livello	level crossing
pensione	boarding houses
pericolo	danger
rallentare	slow down
scheda tecnica	schedule of technical data on a vehicle
senso vietato	no entry
senso unico	one way
sosta autorizzato	parking permitted at certain times
sosta vietato	no parking
strada (privata)	road (private)
uscita	exit
verde	lead-free petrol
Viacard	motorway toll card
vietato ingresso	no entry
zona blu	parking within blue lines only
zona disco	parking within restricted time
zona rimozione	no parking: cars will be towed away
zona tutelato	no parking either side of road

FINANCIAL MATTERS

bollo	chit or state stamp
bonus/malus	insurance policy based on no claims bonuses
buste	payslips
camera di commercio	chamber of commerce
commercialista	book-keeper, accountant
denuncia	statement; income tax return
franchigia	insurance policy with an excess limit
imposte	tax
ricevuta fiscale	receipt
scala mobili	wage indexation
tangenti	kick-backs, bribes
Ufficio Imposte Dirette	Provincial Tax Office

GENERAL

affitasi/da affitare	to rent
agenzia	agent, agency
alimentari	grocery stores
antiquario	antique shop
calzolaio	shoe repairer
Carta Si	an Italian Credit Card
cartolibreria	bookshop
casa del formaggio	cheese shop
casa di pasta	pasta shop
comune, municipio	town hall
denuncia	legal/police statement
elenchi telefonici	telephone directories
enoteca	wine merchant
fai da te	DIY
farmacia	chemist
ferramenta	hardware store
francobolli	postage stamp

gabinetti	WC
gelateria	ice cream shop
macelleria	butcher's shop
mercato	market
omertà	Mafia law of silence
paneficio/panetteria	bakery
parrucchiere	hairdresser
passeggiata	evening stroll or promenade
pescheria	fishmonger
profumeria	perfumery
saldi	sales
signore, signori	ladies, gentlemen
supermercato	supermarket
tabacchi	tobacconists
tintoria	drycleaner
toiletta	WC
Tribunale	Magistrates Court
Ufficio Postale	Post Office
Vigili Urbani	Town Police

Further Reading

GENERAL

Getting a Job Abroad, Roger Jones (How To Books, 7th edn, 2003).
Planning Your Gap Year, Nick Vandome, (How To Books, 6th edn. 2003).
Retire Abroad, Roger Jones (How To Books, 2nd edn, 2003).
Fodor's Italy 2003 (Fodor 2003).

PROPERTY

Doing Business in Italy, Dalbert Hallenstein (BBC Books, 1991).
Buying Property in Italy, Amanda Hinton (How To Books, 2003).
Italian Villas and their Gardens, Edith Wharton (Da Capo Press).

REGIONAL GUIDES

Italy: Insight Guides Series (Discovery Channel 2002).
Southern Italy: Paul Blanchard (Blue Guides, 2000).
Tuscany, Umbria and the Marches, Michael Pauls and Dana Facaros (Cadogan, 2001).
Umbria: Alta Macadam (Blue Guides, 2000).

FOOD AND WINE

Antonio Carluccio's Italian Feast, Antonio Carluccio (BBC Consumer Publishing, 1996).
Pocket Guide to Italian Food and Wine, Spike & Charmian Hughes (Carberry Press, 1992).
Recipes from an Italian Farmhouse, Valentina Harris (Simon & Schuster 1990).

Valentina Harris Cooks Italian, Valentina Harris (BBC Books, 1996).

Vino Italiano: The Regional Wines of Italy, Joseph Bastianich (Clarkson N. Potter 2002).

CITY GUIDES

Florence

Florence, Alta Macadam (Blue Guides: A & C Black, 2001).

Florence: A Literary Companion, Francis King (Penguin Books 2001).

The American Express guide to Florence and Tuscany, Sheila Hale (Mitchell Beazley 1989).

Rome

Rome: Blue City Guide, Alta Macadam (A & C Black, 2000).

Venice

Venice: Blue Guide City Guide, Alta Macadam (A & C Black, 2000).

City Secrets: Florence, Venice and the Towns of Italy, Tim Adams (Robert Kahn, 2001).

ITALIAN CULTURE

Art and Architecture

Art and Architecture in Italy 1250-1400, John White (Yale University Press, 1993).

Architecture of the Italian Renaissance, Peter Murray (Thames & Hudson, 1986).

History of Italian Renaissance Art, Frederick Hartt (Thames & Hudson, 1994).

Italian Renaissance Painting, Keith Roberts (Phaidon, 1993).

Italian Renaissance Sculpture: World of Art Series, Roberta Olson (Thames & Hudson, 1992).

Cinema

Italian Cinema, Peter Bondanella (Roundhouse Publishing, 1999).

Italian Films, Robin Buss (Batsford, 1990).

Design

Italian Interior Design, Laura Andreini (Teneues Publishing UK Ltd).

History

A Traveller's History of Italy, Valerio Lintner (Windrush, 1989).
The Florentine Renaissance, Vincent Cronin (Pimlico, 1992).
The Italian Renaissance, J. H. Plumb (Houghton Mifflin, 1990).
Italy: A Short History, Harry Hearder (Cambridge University Press, 1991).

Literature

Italian Short Stories (No. 1), R. Trevelyan (Penguin, 1965).
Italian Short Stories (No. 2), D. Vittorini (Penguin, 1972).
Italian Stories in English and Italian, Robert Hall (Dover, 1990).

Music

Italian Opera, David R B Kimbell (CUP 1994).
Famous Italian Opera Arias, Ellen H Bleiler (Dover Publications 1996).
Italian Folk Song and Music, Luisa Del Guidice (Garland Science 2000).

Index